Albertina's

Exceptional Recipes

This book is dedicated to the many volunteers who work faith-
fully and cheerfully in the kitchen and dining room as well as
behind the scenes at Albertina's. Our heartfelt thanks to all of
you who have given so much of yourselves in a volunteer labor
of love.

ALBERTINA'S EXCEPTIONAL RECIPES is a collection of new and old favorites that have been carefully tested. A number of our most requested recipes from ALBERTINA'S COOKBOOKS I and II, which are no longer in print, are included, together with more than a hundred new recipes. All have been used in our restaurant. The collection, compiled by our Cookbook Committee, is proudly presented for your enjoyment.

<u>THE COMMITTEE</u>

Berth Guptill and Ann North, Chairpersons

Barbara Crampton	Nancy Hughes
Blanche Crook	Rea Janes
Beth Gerber	Emily Nelson
Jane Goudy	Georgie Packwood

Virginia Williamson

We sincerely thank Ann Armstrong and Lillian Pierce for their professional advice and assistance and especially for their patience, care and unfailing good humor.

A special thank you to the many volunteers who have contributed and served on the Menu Committee for ALBERTINA'S over the years.

Copyright 1996 by Albertina's
First Published in October 1996
Second Printing October 1997
Third Printing August 1999
Fourth Printing November 2002
Fifth Printing January 2008
ISBN 0-9654691-0-7
Library of Congress Catalog Card Number 96-86742

Typesetting and graphics: Leslie Harris Graphic Design; Opus Design
Printed by: ADPRINT Company
Bindery: Lincoln & Allen

To order additional copies of Albertina's Exceptional Recipes, please refer to the information provided in the back of the book.

All proceeds from the cookbook go to the Albertina Kerr Centers.

Albertina's
at the Old Kerr Nursery

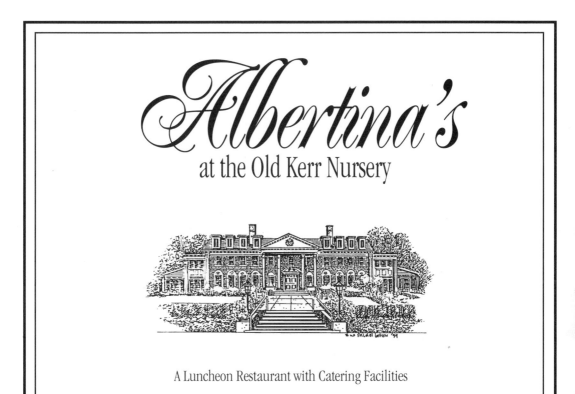

A Luncheon Restaurant with Catering Facilities

The Kerr Nursery on Northeast 22nd Avenue served as a Portland orphanage and nursery from 1921 until 1967. The Nursery's establishment was the result of the work and concern of Alexander Kerr, developer and manufacturer of the Kerr Jar and Lid. For fifty-five years, the Kerr Nursery provided shelter and medical care to approximately two hundred children per year. The nursery closed its doors in 1967 and in 1979 the building was listed in the National Register of Historic Places. Albertina's at the Old Kerr Nursery, opened in 1981.

Albertina's
424 N.E. 22nd Ave.
Portland, OR 97232
(503) 231-0216

Our restaurant bears the name of ALBERTINA, the beautiful young wife of Alexander Kerr. Albertina's dying request was that a home for orphan children be established and, to honor that request, Alexander donated their home on southwest 14th street for the care of abandoned children. The Kerr home became the first Albertina Kerr Nursery Home, opening in December, 1912. Through the years, the organization has evolved into a multi-service agency responding to critical community needs.

Proceeds from the restaurant support the Albertina Kerr Centers and all gratuities are forwarded each month directly to the Centers' programs.

Contents

Soups

In 1978, an ongoing volunteer effort began, dedicated to the renovation of The Old Kerr Nursery building on Northeast 22nd Avenue. Today, the first floor of the building is occupied by three businesses: Albertina's, a luncheon restaurant; The Kerr Gift Shop, which features unique gifts; and Kerr's Economy Jar, where outstanding treasures from the past can be found. A separate building houses the Thrift Shop, which is stocked with donated items of fine quality. Fashion shows from the Thrift Shop are featured at Albertina's luncheons frequently. All businesses are managed and staffed by volunteers, with proceeds donated to Albertina Kerr Centers.

CURRIED ASPARAGUS SOUP

2 tablespoons butter

1 leek, cleaned and sliced (white part only)

4 cups chicken broth

2 medium potatoes, peeled and diced

2 (1-pound) cans asparagus, including liquid

2 teaspoons curry powder

1/8 teaspoon white pepper

Croutons

Serves 10.

Sauté leek in butter for 5 minutes. Add chicken broth, potatoes, asparagus, curry and pepper. Simmer 20-30 minutes.

Puree in food processor. Return to pan and reheat. Taste for seasonings and add more curry, pepper or salt if needed. Garnish with croutons.

FRESH BROCCOLI SOUP

A creamy and delicious soup without the calories

4 tablespoons vegetable oil

1 medium onion, diced

1 medium potato, diced

2/3 cup diced celery

1 clove garlic, minced

5 cups chicken broth

1/2 teaspoon salt

1/4 teaspoon white pepper

4 tablespoons fresh basil or 1 1/2 teaspoons dried

1 large stalk broccoli, cut in 1-inch pieces

2 tablespoons lemon juice

Lemon slices

Serves 8-10.

Sauté all vegetables except broccoli in oil for 10 minutes over medium heat. Add chicken broth and seasonings. Cover and cook slowly for 10 minutes. Add stem pieces of broccoli and cook for 5 minutes. Add remaining broccoli and cook for 5 minutes longer or until broccoli is barely tender.

Puree soup in food processor or blender. Return soup to pan, and just before serving add lemon juice and reheat. Taste and add more salt, if needed. Float a thin slice of lemon on top of each serving.

CURRIED CARROT SOUP

2 tablespoons olive oil

2 medium onions, chopped

1 cup chopped celery

5 cups chicken broth

1½ pounds carrots, chopped or grated

1 pound russet potatoes, peeled and cut into 1-inch chunks

1 teaspoon ground cumin

1 teaspoon curry powder

3 tablespoons lemon juice

WATERCRESS PURÉE

1 cup lightly packed watercress sprigs

¼ cup plain yogurt

Serves 8-10.

In a 4-5 quart saucepan, heat oil over medium heat. Sauté onions and celery for 5 minutes. Add chicken broth, then add carrots, potatoes, cumin and curry. Simmer, covered, until potatoes are tender when pierced (about 10-20 minutes). Add lemon juice.

Blend hot soup, a portion at a time, in a food processor, leaving soup with a slightly chunky texture. Return to pan and reheat.

When ready to serve, pour into bowls and drizzle Watercress Purée over the top or sprinkle with chopped parsley.

To make Watercress Purée, puree the watercress in a food processor. Add the yogurt and blend together.

SUNSET CARROT SOUP

Bay leaf is the secret to this outstanding soup

4 carrots, peeled and minced

1 onion, minced

4 tablespoons butter

1 tablespoon flour

3 cups chicken broth

1 bay leaf

½ cup half and half

Salt and pepper to taste

Chopped parsley or carrot curls

Serves 6.

Cook carrots and onion in butter (do not brown). Stir in flour. Gradually add broth and bring to simmer. Add bay leaf and simmer for 30 minutes. Remove bay leaf, place in food processor. Add half and half and seasonings and blend until smooth. To serve, reheat and garnish with parsley or carrot curls, if desired.

FRESH MUSHROOM SOUP

A favorite at Albertina's

2 tablespoons butter

2 medium onions, chopped

½ pound fresh mushrooms, sliced

4 cups chicken broth

½ cup chopped parsley

3 tablespoons tomato paste

1 clove garlic, minced

¼ teaspoon pepper

½ cup white wine

Serves 6-8.

Sauté onion in butter until almost tender, then add mushrooms and sauté briefly. Add broth and remaining ingredients, except wine, and bring to boil. Reduce heat, add wine and simmer 5 minutes.

MUSHROOM BISQUE

This soup is even better the next day

½ pound mushrooms, finely chopped

¼ cup butter

¼ cup flour

¼ teaspoon dry mustard

2 cups chicken broth

2 cups half and half

⅓ cup minced chives

⅓ cup sherry (optional)

Salt

Serves 6.

In saucepan, melt butter and sauté mushrooms until soft. Combine flour and mustard and stir into sautéed mushrooms. Cook for 2 minutes. Add chicken broth and cook until thickened, stirring frequently. Add half and half, sherry and chives, reserving some chives for garnish. Taste and add salt, if needed.

PIMIENTO BISQUE

The delicate flavor will surprise you

1 (4-ounce) jar pimiento,
   drained

2½ cups chicken broth, divided

¼ cup butter

¼ cup flour

⅛ teaspoon pepper

1½ cups half and half

Chopped parsley or chives
   (optional)

Serves 4-6.

In a blender or food processor, puree pimiento and 1 cup of chicken broth. Set aside. In a medium saucepan, melt butter. Stir in flour and pepper. Cook on medium heat until bubbly, about 3 minutes. Gradually add 1½ cups chicken broth, half and half and blended pimiento, stirring constantly. Simmer, stirring frequently, until bisque is slightly thickened and piping hot. Taste and add salt as needed. Garnish with chopped parsley or chives.

SAVORY TOMATO SOUP

How can a soup so easily made be so good?

12 green onions, chopped

3 large cloves of garlic, minced

4 cups tomato juice

1 (28-ounce) can crushed
   tomatoes

2 tablespoons brown sugar

1 teaspoon salt

⅛ teaspoon pepper

½ cup sour cream

Serves 8.

Put onion, garlic and tomato juice in saucepan. Cook over medium heat for 15 minutes. Add tomatoes, brown sugar, salt and pepper. Cook, covered, for 15 minutes. Serve hot, garnished with sour cream.

SUNRISE TOMATO SOUP

2 tablespoons butter or
   margarine

2 tablespoons olive oil

2 cups chopped onion

3/4 teaspoon thyme

1 1/4 teaspoons basil

1/8 teaspoon pepper

3 1/2 cups canned Italian
   tomatoes

3 tablespoons tomato paste

3 3/4 cups chicken broth

4 tablespoons flour

1/3 cup cold water

1 teaspoon granulated sugar

1 cup half and half

Sour cream and chives
   (optional)

Serves 8-10.

Melt butter in saucepan then add olive oil, onion, thyme, basil and pepper. Sauté until onion is transparent. Add tomatoes, tomato paste and broth. Simmer 30 minutes, stirring often to prevent burning. Purée soup in blender or food processor. Return to heat.

Blend flour and cold water and add to soup, stirring constantly. Add sugar and half and half. Simmer 5 more minutes or until hot and thickened. Taste and add salt, if needed. Garnish with a dollop of sour cream and chives if desired.

TOMATO CONSOMMÉ

2 cups chicken broth

3/4 cup tomato juice

1/8 teaspoon garlic salt

1 teaspoon sugar

1/8 teaspoon ground white
   pepper

1/4 teaspoon basil

1/2 cup white wine

Serves 4.

Combine all ingredients, except wine, in a saucepan. Bring to a boil and then simmer for 5 minutes. Add wine just before serving and reheat.

Vegetable Consommé

2 cups vegetable juice (V-8)

1¾ cups beef broth

1¼ teaspoons sugar

2½ tablespoons lemon juice

1½ teaspoons Worcestershire sauce

Pepper to taste

Topping

⅓ cup sour cream

2 teaspoons snipped fresh chives

½ teaspoon lemon juice

Serves 4.

Heat juice and broth to boiling. Add other ingredients and simmer 5-10 minutes.

To make topping, combine sour cream, chives and lemon juice. Mix well and chill. Garnish each serving with a spoonful of topping.

CHICKEN SOUP WITH WATER CHESTNUTS

A modern mom's chicken soup — with a crunch

6 cups chicken broth

2 cups cooked chicken, diced
(or cut into thin strips)

1 (8-ounce) can sliced water
chestnuts, drained

¼ pound mushrooms, sliced

1 tablespoon cornstarch

2 tablespoons cold water

2 tablespoons sherry

¼ teaspoon sesame oil

Salt

Chopped green onions or
parsley for garnish

Serves 8.

Bring chicken broth to a boil in a large saucepan. Add diced chicken, water chestnuts and mushrooms. Reduce heat to low, cover the pan and simmer 5 minutes. Blend cornstarch and water together. Add sherry and cornstarch mixture to soup. Cook over medium-high heat, stirring constantly, until soup thickens slightly. Stir in the sesame oil. Taste and add salt if needed. Garnish with chopped green onions or parsley.

QUICK AND EASY GAZPACHO

A smooth alternative to an old-time favorite

1 (46-ounce) can vegetable juice (V-8)

3 tablespoons red wine vinegar

¼ teaspoon white pepper

⅛ teaspoon garlic powder

¾ teaspoon celery salt

¼ teaspoon Tabasco

½ small onion

½ medium green pepper

1½ medium cucumbers, peeled, seeded and cut in large pieces

2 ribs celery, cut in large pieces

8 pimiento-stuffed olives

Chopped green onions or parsley (optional)

Serves 8-10.

Combine vegetable juice with red wine vinegar, white pepper, garlic powder, celery salt and Tabasco.

Put ½ of the vegetable juice mixture into food processor. Add onion, green pepper, cucumber, celery and olives. Blend mixture well. Pour blended gazpacho into remaining vegetable juice. Mix well and chill. Garnish with chopped green onions or parsley, if desired.

GAZPACHO

2½ cups tomato juice

3 tablespoons white wine vinegar

3 tablespoons olive oil

2 tablespoons lemon juice

1 teaspoon Worcestershire sauce

Tabasco, few drops

¼ teaspoon pepper

½ teaspoon salt

4 large, very ripe tomatoes, peeled and chopped

1 large cucumber, peeled, seeded and chopped

1 medium onion, minced

1 green pepper, diced

1 cup chopped celery

1 clove garlic, finely chopped

Sour cream (optional)

Chopped parsley (optional)

Serves 12.

Combine liquids and seasonings. Add prepared vegetables and mix well. Chill overnight. Serve in chilled glass bowls and garnish with a dollop of sour cream or fresh chopped parsley.

CHILLED ZUCCHINI SOUP

An unusually delicious soup from your garden's bounty

¼ cup butter

4 cups chopped onions

1 clove garlic, minced

3 pounds zucchini, cut into 1-
inch cubes (don't peel)

4 cups chicken broth

1 teaspoon curry powder

⅛ teaspoon powdered ginger

½ teaspoon salt

¼ teaspoon white pepper

1 teaspoon sugar

¼ cup lemon juice

2 cups sour cream

Paprika (optional)

Chopped parsley (optional)

Serves 10.

Melt butter in large stock pot. Sauté onion and garlic in butter until transparent. Add zucchini and cook 5-10 minutes, stirring often. Add chicken broth, all seasonings and lemon juice. Simmer 10-15 minutes or until zucchini is tender, but not mushy.

Purée in food processor in small batches. Chill thoroughly. Add sour cream and mix well.

Serve in chilled bowls with a sprinkle of paprika, topped with a small amount of chopped parsley, if desired.

ICED CUCUMBER SOUP

Refreshing on a hot summer evening

3 cucumbers, peeled and
   seeded

3 large green onions, white part
   only, chopped

2 tablespoons butter

1 tablespoon flour

3 cups chicken broth

1 bay leaf

1 cup sour cream

1 tablespoon lemon juice

1 teaspoon dill weed

White pepper

Salt

Serves 8.

Chop 2 cucumbers and sauté with the onions in butter. Stir in flour. Gradually add broth and bring to a simmer. Add bay leaf and cook for 20 minutes, stirring occasionally. Remove bay leaf and purée mixture in food processor or blender. Chill.

Grate remaining cucumber. Add cucumber, lemon juice, dill weed and sour cream to chilled, pureed soup. Taste and add salt and pepper, if needed. Serve very cold.

WILD RICE CLAM CHOWDER

Extraordinary clam chowder

6½ cups chicken broth

1 tablespoon lemon juice

3 whole bay leaves

6 medium red potatoes, cut into
   ½-inch cubes

1½ cups chopped onions

¼ cup butter

6 ounces fresh mushrooms,
   sliced

2 (6½-ounce) cans minced
   clams, with juice

½ teaspoon pepper

⅓ cup flour

1½ cups half and half

2½ cups cooked wild rice

Serves 12.

Bring chicken broth, lemon juice and bay leaves to a boil in a large kettle. Add potatoes and simmer 10-15 minutes or until just tender.

While potatoes are cooking, sauté onions in butter until transparent, but do not brown. Add mushrooms to onions and sauté 5-10 minutes more. Add onions and mushrooms and their liquid to potatoes and broth. Add clams, juice and pepper. Heat chowder.

Mix flour with ½ cup half and half to make a smooth paste. Slowly add flour mixture to chowder, stirring well to avoid lumping. Add remaining half and half and cooked wild rice. Heat to piping hot.

SEAFOOD BISQUE

Perfect with a fresh green salad and PANTRY CHEESE BREAD

2 (6-ounce) cans chopped clams

1¼ cups chicken broth

1½ cups tomato juice

½ cup dry white wine

2 tablespoons dry sherry

½ teaspoon oregano

3 large ripe tomatoes, peeled, seeded and chopped or 2 cups diced canned tomatoes

3 cloves garlic, minced

4 drops Tabasco

1 cup half and half

1 pound white fish fillets, cut in bite-size pieces

¼ pound scallops

¼ pound shrimp

1 cup finely chopped parsley

Serves 8-10.

In a 4-5 quart pan, combine clams and liquid, chicken broth, tomato juice, wine, sherry, oregano, tomatoes, garlic and Tabasco. Bring to a boil over high heat. Reduce heat, cover and simmer until tomatoes are soft (about 5 minutes). Pour half and half into a bowl. Pour 1 cup of the hot tomato mixture slowly into the half and half, stirring well. Slowly pour this mixture back into the pan of hot soup. Heat bisque on low heat. Just before serving, add pieces of white fish. Simmer for 3-4 minutes or until fish is opaque. Add shrimp and scallops and heat 3-5 minutes more. Stir in chopped parsley and serve.

PRECIOUS ITEM SOUP

Inspiring combination of vegetables, meat and seafood

6 cups chicken broth

1 tablespoon soy sauce

1 teaspoon sugar

⅛ teaspoon sesame oil

3 tablespoons cornstarch

¼ cup cold water

1 cup sliced bok choy

⅓ pound mushrooms, sliced

½ cup canned sliced bamboo shoots, drained

½ cup sliced water chestnuts

1 cup thinly sliced cooked chicken breast

1 cup sliced snow peas (1-inch lengths)

1 cup cooked bay shrimp

Chow mein noodles

Serves 8-10.

In soup kettle, heat chicken broth, soy sauce, sugar and sesame oil.

Mix together cornstarch and cold water to make a smooth paste. Slowly add to hot broth, stirring well.

Cut bok choy slices from the stem end, slicing thinly on the diagonal. Add bok choy, mushrooms, bamboo shoots, water chestnuts and chicken to soup. Simmer over medium-low heat until vegetables are tender.

Just before serving, add snow peas and shrimp (larger shrimp may be used if desired). Ladle into bowls. Garnish with chow mein noodles at the very last minute.

COLONY CHICKEN SOUP

An old favorite — the sauerkraut makes it special

2½ pounds chicken pieces

6 cups water

4 teaspoons chicken base or 4 chicken bouillon cubes

1 cup chopped celery

1 cup grated carrots

1 cup chopped onions

¼ cup melted butter

¼ cup flour

1½ cups half and half or milk

¼ teaspoon white pepper

2 cups sauerkraut, rinsed, drained and chopped

Serves 8-10.

In a large kettle, simmer chicken in water to which chicken base or bouillon cubes have been added, being careful not to boil. When chicken is cooked through and tender, about 30-45 minutes, remove chicken. When cool, skin, debone and cut into bite-size pieces and set aside to add later. Degrease broth.

Add celery, carrots and onions to chicken broth. Simmer about 12 minutes or until tender.

Mix melted butter and flour. Gradually add to broth, stirring well. Add half and half and white pepper. Stir frequently until soup is very hot and slightly thickened. Add sauerkraut and chicken pieces. Simmer on very low heat for a few minutes before serving. The flavor of this delicious soup becomes even better when served the second day.

WINTER BEEF BURGUNDY SOUP

A hearty soup on a wintry night

2 onions, chopped

2 tablespoons butter

1 pound lean ground beef

1 clove garlic, minced

4 cups beef broth

4 cups diced tomatoes with juice

1½ cups diced potatoes

1 cup diced celery

1 cup cut green beans

1 cup sliced carrots

1 cup Burgundy wine

2 tablespoons chopped parsley

½ teaspoon basil

¼ teaspoon thyme

1 teaspoon salt

½ teaspoon pepper

Serves 10-12.

In large kettle, cook onions in butter until tender. Add ground beef and garlic and cook until meat has browned. Add remaining ingredients and simmer for 1 hour. Taste and add more salt, if needed.

This soup is better when made ahead and reheated.

ASPARAGUS LEEK CHOWDER

A seasonal favorite

½ pound mushrooms, sliced

2 large leeks, sliced

1 (10-ounce) package frozen, cut asparagus or equal amount of fresh, cut

6 tablespoons butter

3 tablespoons flour

½ teaspoon salt

⅛ teaspoon pepper

2 cups chicken broth

2 cups half and half

1 (12-ounce) can white whole-kernel corn, undrained

2 tablespoons chopped pimiento

Serves 6-8.

Over low heat, cook mushrooms, leeks and asparagus in butter until almost tender (about 10 minutes). Stir in flour, salt and pepper. Add chicken broth and simmer 10 minutes. Add half and half and heat, stirring constantly, until hot and bubbly. Stir in corn and pimiento and heat through, being careful not to boil. Season to taste with additional salt and pepper, if needed.

JARLSBERG VEGETABLE SOUP

4 cups chicken broth

¾ cup grated carrots

½ cup chopped celery

½ cup chopped onion

1 small clove garlic, minced

¼ teaspoon thyme, crushed

¼ teaspoon salt

⅛ teaspoon white pepper

2 cups coarsely chopped
   broccoli

1 cup half and half

¼ cup margarine or butter

⅓ cup flour

1½ cups grated Jarlsberg or
   Swiss cheese

Serves 6-8.

In a 4-quart heavy saucepan add all the vegetables, except broccoli, to the chicken broth. Add seasonings and cover. Simmer until vegetables are almost tender. Add broccoli and simmer 3 minutes.

Gradually add half and half to vegetables and broth. In a small pan, melt margarine and add flour, stirring well. Slowly add to soup mixture, stirring constantly until soup has thickened slightly. Stir in cheese and serve.

Salads

The Old Kerr Nursery Association is an umbrella organization supporting the work of its members and the three volunteer operated and managed businesses. The Association also endeavors to perpetuate the historical significance of The Old Kerr Nursery and to improve and maintain the Nursery building and its grounds as a National Historic landmark.

Apple Salad with Chutney Dressing

3 red apples, unpeeled, cored and diced

½ cup golden raisins

⅓ cup thinly sliced green onions

½ cup Spanish peanuts

6 - 8 cups spinach or mixed greens

Chutney Dressing

¼ cup white wine vinegar

2 tablespoons chopped chutney

1 teaspoon curry powder

½ teaspoon salt

1 teaspoon dry mustard

1½ teaspoons sugar

¼ teaspoon Tabasco

1 cup salad oil

Serves 8.

To make dressing, place all ingredients, except oil, in food processor. Blend well. Slowly pour oil into processor as ingredients are mixing. Dressing will thicken. Refrigerate at least 2 hours to allow flavors to blend.

Combine diced apples, raisins and green onions. Coat with part of the dressing. Mix some dressing with the greens and add the rest to the apple mixture. Arrange greens on individual plates. Add peanuts to apple mixture and mound in the center of each plate.

PINEAPPLE WALDORF SALAD

2 red apples, unpeeled, cored
   and diced

¼ cup chopped celery

¼ cup golden raisins

1 cup pineapple tidbits, well
   drained and chilled

¼ cup coarsely chopped
   walnuts

Lettuce leaves

Nutmeg

DRESSING

⅓ cup mayonnaise

2 teaspoons sugar

Serves 6.

Combine dressing ingredients. Pour over apples, mixing gently. Add celery and raisins. Combine and refrigerate. Just before serving, add pineapple and walnuts. Serve on a lettuce leaf. Sprinkle each serving with a dash of nutmeg.

BROCCOLI ALMOND SALAD

1 pound broccoli florets, cut in
   bite-size pieces

1 green pepper, diced

¼ cup chopped onion

⅓ cup Italian dressing

½ cup Parmesan cheese

Lettuce leaves

½ cup toasted slivered almonds

Serves 6-8.

Steam broccoli florets 2-4 minutes or until they become bright green in color. Cool quickly under cold water. Drain well and let dry a few minutes.

Combine the broccoli, green pepper, onion and Italian dressing.

When serving, add Parmesan cheese and serve on a lettuce leaf. Garnish with toasted almonds.

Broccoli Toss

6 cups chopped fresh broccoli
   florets

2 tablespoons chopped onion

4 large mushrooms, sliced

⅓ cup golden raisins

6 - 8 slices of bacon, fried crisp
   and crumbled

Dressing

2 tablespoons cider vinegar

3 ounces cream cheese

2 tablespoons sugar

Dash of pepper

⅛ teaspoon garlic salt

¼ teaspoon salt

1 tablespoon prepared yellow
   mustard

2 tablespoons milk

2 tablespoons salad oil

Serves 8.

To make dressing, mix all dressing ingredients in a blender or food processor. Refrigerate several hours to allow flavors to blend. If dressing is too thick, thin with more milk.

Lightly mix the broccoli, onion, mushrooms and raisins. Pour chilled dressing over vegetables. Toss to mix thoroughly and refrigerate. Add bacon just before serving.

For variation, you may substitute some cauliflower florets for broccoli in this mixture to give contrast in color.

CRUNCHY CONFETTI SALAD

An easy do-ahead combination

1 pound broccoli, cut into small
   florets

1 head cauliflower, cut into
   small florets

4 green onions, chopped

4 medium carrots, cut into ⅛-
   inch diagonal slices

8 slices bacon, cooked crisp,
   drained and crumbled

Chopped parsley for garnish

Green-leaf lettuce

DRESSING

½ cup mayonnaise

¼ cup tarragon wine vinegar

⅓ cup sugar

Serves 10-12.

To prepare dressing, combine all dressing
ingredients and mix well. You may want to
reserve a little dressing to add to the top
when serving.

Place first 4 vegetables in a bowl. Add
dressing and toss. Chill several hours or
overnight. Drain excess dressing before
serving. Add crumbled bacon. Serve on
green-leaf lettuce and sprinkle with
chopped parsley.

Fresh Carrot Salad

1 pound carrots, shredded

1 green pepper, diced

½ cup chopped onion

1 red delicious apple, cored
and grated

1 cup golden raisins

Green-leaf lettuce

Green pepper strips

DRESSING

⅓ cup cider vinegar

¼ cup salad oil

3 tablespoons sugar

½ teaspoon celery seed

½ teaspoon dry mustard

½ teaspoon salt

Serves 8-10.

Mix dressing ingredients in a small saucepan and bring to a boil. Cool.

Combine carrots, green pepper, onion, apple and raisins. Add dressing. Refrigerate at least 2 hours. Drain. Serve mounded on green-leaf lettuce. Garnish with green pepper strips.

COLESLAW WITH PEAS AND PEANUTS

1 (10-ounce) package frozen peas, thawed

2 cups finely shredded cabbage

1 green onion, finely sliced

¼ cup sour cream

¼ cup mayonnaise

¼ teaspoon curry powder

¼ teaspoon salt

⅛ teaspoon pepper

1 teaspoon prepared mustard

1 teaspoon white wine vinegar

½ cup chopped salted peanuts

Serves 6.

In a salad bowl, mix together peas, cabbage and onion.

In a small bowl, mix remaining ingredients except peanuts. Pour over cabbage mixture and toss lightly. Cover and refrigerate for at least 1 hour or overnight.

Garnish with peanuts before serving.

CRUNCHY PEA SALAD

The best pea salad yet

1 (10-ounce) package petite
    frozen peas, thawed

1 cup diced celery

¼ cup chopped green onion

¾ cup chopped salted cashews
    or macadamia nuts

¼ cup crumbled, crisply fried
    bacon

DRESSING

1 cup sour cream

¼ cup Italian garlic dressing

½ teaspoon salt

Serves 6.

To prepare dressing, combine all dressing
ingredients and chill.

Combine peas, celery and green onions.
Add ½ cup dressing and chill. At serving
time, add nuts, bacon and more dressing.
Serve on a lettuce leaf.

NOTE: Chopped water chestnuts make a
nice crunchy substitute for celery.

MUSHROOM WALNUT SALAD

Fennel seed adds a unique flavor

1 medium head of Romaine, cut
   in bite-size pieces

½ pound mushrooms, sliced

1 cup chopped toasted walnuts

DRESSING

½ cup olive oil

3 tablespoons red wine vinegar

1 clove garlic, minced

½ teaspoon salt

½ teaspoon ground fennel seed

1 hard-cooked egg

Freshly ground pepper, to taste

Serves 8.

To prepare dressing, combine all dressing ingredients, except egg and pepper. Store at room temperature.

At serving time, place lettuce on salad plates and arrange mushrooms on top. Blend the dressing mixture in a food processor. Cut the egg in pieces, and add to mixture. Blend well. Grind pepper into dressing. Drizzle over lettuce and mushrooms and sprinkle with walnuts.

Fresh Mushroom Salad

Mushrooms all dressed up for company

½ pound mushrooms, sliced

½ head iceberg lettuce, torn

½ head green-leaf lettuce or
  Romaine lettuce, torn

Red pepper strips for garnish

Mustard Vinaigrette

2 tablespoons Dijon mustard

1½ tablespoons white wine
  vinegar

1 clove garlic, minced

1 teaspoon sugar

¼ teaspoon salt

¼ teaspoon pepper

⅓ cup salad oil

¼ cup sour cream

Serves 6.

Place all dressing ingredients except oil and sour cream in food processor. Blend well. Slowly add oil while machine is running. Dressing will thicken. Set aside for flavors to blend.

Clean and tear greens and refrigerate.

Add about ⅓ cup dressing to sliced mushrooms. Mix and set aside. Add sour cream to remaining dressing.

At serving time, toss greens with dressing. (Dressing may be thinned with milk if it is too thick.) Divide greens evenly on serving plates, and place marinated mushrooms on top of each salad. Garnish with strips of red pepper.

MANDARIN ORANGE SALAD WITH GINGER DRESSING

2 heads Romaine lettuce, chilled

2 (11-ounce) cans Mandarin oranges, well drained

1 small can sliced ripe olives, well drained

GINGER DRESSING

1 clove garlic

2 tablespoons finely grated fresh ginger

1 cup white wine vinegar

¼ cup fresh lemon juice

1 tablespoon grated lemon peel

1 cup sugar

1 tablespoon catsup

1 cup oil

Serves 8.

To prepare Ginger Dressing, use a food processor and steel blade, dropping garlic clove through feed tube while processor is running. Add remaining dressing ingredients except oil. Mix well. With machine running, slowly add oil. Refrigerate to meld flavors.

Tear lettuce in bite-sized pieces and place into salad bowl. Toss with enough dressing to coat leaves. Add some dressing to oranges and olives. Divide salad on serving plates. Garnish each serving with orange-olive mixture.

ORANGE POPPY-SEED SALAD

Irresistible!

- 1 - 2 heads (5 - 6 cups) Romaine or butter lettuce
- 2 - 3 oranges, peeled and sectioned
- ¼ cup bleu cheese, crumbled
- 1 avocado, diced
- 3 tablespoons toasted pine nuts or slivered almonds

DRESSING

- ¼ cup sugar
- 1 teaspoon salt
- 1 teaspoon dry mustard
- ½ small red onion
- ½ cup cider vinegar
- 1 cup vegetable oil
- 2 tablespoons poppy seeds

Serves 6.

To prepare dressing, mix all dressing ingredients except oil and seeds and pulse several times. Slowly pour oil through feed tube while machine is running. Add poppy seeds last.

Tear lettuce into bite-size pieces. Place in bowl. Add oranges, cheese and avocado and toss. Add enough dressing to coat and toss well (you will have dressing left over). Sprinkle pine nuts over salad and serve.

SALAD COQUILLE

A perfect compliment to any meal

- 1 head of iceberg lettuce, torn in bite-size pieces
- 1 head of leaf lettuce, torn in bite-size pieces
- 1 cup Mandarin oranges, drained
- 4 red onion slices, separated into rings
- ¼ cup slivered almonds, toasted

DRESSING

- 2½ tablespoons white wine vinegar
- ½ tablespoon lemon juice
- ½ teaspoon dry mustard
- ½ teaspoon paprika
- 2½ tablespoons honey
- ⅓ cup sugar
- ½ teaspoon celery salt
- ½ teaspoon grated onion
- ½ cup salad oil

Serves 8-10.

To prepare dressing, heat all dressing ingredients, except oil, until sugar dissolves. Add oil and cool mixture. Before serving, whisk or blend dressing thoroughly.

Layer lettuce, oranges and onions in a salad bowl. Toss with dressing when ready to serve. Sprinkle with toasted almonds.

SALAD BOWL

We're nuts about this Albertina's classic

7 - 8 cups mixed greens, torn in
    bite-size pieces (may include
    Bibb lettuce, spinach, etc.)

2 green onions, chopped

¼ cup sliced celery

1 cup Mandarin oranges,
    drained (or sliced fresh
    orange)

½ cup caramelized walnuts

DRESSING

½ cup salad oil

Salt and pepper to taste

¼ cup parsley, chopped

2 tablespoons sugar

2 tablespoons cider vinegar

Dash of Tabasco or red pepper

CARAMELIZED WALNUTS

½ cup walnuts, chopped
    coarsely

3 tablespoons sugar

Serves 8.

Make dressing by mixing all dressing ingredients. Set aside to allow flavors to blend. Whisk or blend just before using.

Make caramelized walnuts by slowly heating sugar in a heavy skillet until it melts and becomes a light caramel color. Quickly stir in walnuts, coating well. Immediately turn into a well-greased pan. Cool and break pieces apart. Caramelized nuts will be very hot at first.

At serving time, toss greens, celery and onions with whisked dressing. Divide on eight plates. Top with oranges and sprinkle with caramelized walnuts.

GREENS JULIUS

Albertina's answer to Caesar salad

1 head of Romaine lettuce

½ bunch spinach leaves or
    green-leaf lettuce

½ cup grated Parmesan cheese

1 cup croutons

DRESSING

⅓ cup vegetable oil

2 tablespoons olive oil

2 tablespoons white wine
    vinegar

3 tablespoons fresh lemon juice

1 clove garlic, minced

2 teaspoons minced fresh chives

¾ teaspoon salt

¼ teaspoon fresh ground
    pepper

1 teaspoon Dijon mustard

½ teaspoon Maggi seasoning

CROUTONS

5 slices of fresh bread

¼ cup melted butter

⅛ teaspoon garlic powder

2 - 3 drops Maggi seasoning

Serves 6-8.

Prepare dressing by placing all dressing ingredients in a bowl or jar. Mix well. Ingredients will separate. Store at room temperature. Just before using, beat or shake well.

Wash, dry and cut greens into bite-sized pieces. Refrigerate to crisp. Just before serving, place greens in a large salad bowl. Add just enough salad dressing to coat greens well. Toss gently. Sprinkle Parmesan cheese over greens and toss again. Top with croutons.

To prepare croutons, remove crusts from bread and cut into small cubes. Combine garlic powder and Maggi seasoning with melted butter. Toss seasoned butter with bread cubes, coating well. Place on baking sheet and bake at 350 degrees for 10-15 minutes, stirring frequently. Croutons are done when they are crispy and golden brown. Cool.

TUSCANY GREEN SALAD

Peppery feta sets the stage for a Mediterranean feast

6 cups fresh mixed greens

1 cup peeled sliced cucumber

½ large red pepper, cut into strips

½ cup thinly sliced red onion rings

12 kalamata Greek or Italian olives, pitted and cut in halves

½ cup crumbled black-peppercorn feta cheese

ITALIAN VINAIGRETTE

⅓ cup olive oil

2 tablespoons red wine vinegar

1 tablespoon fresh lemon juice

½ teaspoon salt

½ teaspoon granulated sugar

2 cloves garlic, minced

½ teaspoon dried oregano, crumbled

¼ teaspoon medium-grind black pepper

¼ teaspoon dried Italian seasoning

½ teaspoon Dijon mustard

Serves 6.

To prepare Italian Vinaigrette, whisk together oil, vinegar, lemon juice, salt and sugar in a small bowl. Add garlic, herbs, pepper and mustard. Stir well before serving.

Layer first four ingredients in order listed. Just before serving, toss with Italian Vinaigrette. Add olives and feta cheese.

You may add freshly ground pepper to regular feta cheese if you cannot find peppercorn feta cheese.

Spinach Salad with Roasted Hazelnuts

Oregon hazelnuts add a special touch to this fascinating combination

1 pound (2 bunches) fresh
    spinach leaves or a mixture
    of spinach and green-leaf
    lettuce or Romaine

¼ pound fresh mushrooms,
    sliced

4 slices bacon, diced and
    crisply fried

½ cup chopped toasted
    hazelnuts

Dressing

¼ cup olive oil

3 tablespoons fresh lemon juice

1 tablespoon Dijon mustard

¼ teaspoon freshly ground
    pepper

2 teaspoons honey

1 teaspoon Worcestershire
    sauce

½ teaspoon salt

Serves 4-6.

To prepare dressing, combine all dressing ingredients. Mix well and store at room temperature.

Wash and dry spinach and other greens. Cut spinach or Romaine (tear green-leaf) into small pieces. Place in salad bowl and add mushrooms.

Just before serving, thoroughly mix dressing and add enough to coat greens and mushrooms. Toss well. Gently mix in bacon pieces. Garnish with hazelnuts.

NOTE: To toast hazelnuts, spread the shelled nuts in a shallow pan and toast in oven at 275 degrees for 20-30 minutes or until skins crack. To remove skins, rub nuts while warm with a rough cloth.

Spinach Almond Salad

This salad is excellent as a summer accompaniment to baked chicken or other meat entrées

6 cups washed, torn spinach leaves

3 cups cold, cooked long-grain rice

½ cup thinly sliced red onion

8 slices bacon, crisply fried and crumbled

Pepper, freshly ground

¼ cup sliced toasted almonds

Almond Dressing

⅓ cup salad oil

¼ cup red wine vinegar

1 tablespoon sugar

1 teaspoon dry mustard

¼ teaspoon almond extract

Serves 8.

Prepare Almond Dressing by combining all dressing ingredients.

Combine rice, onion and dressing. Refrigerate.

At serving time, add bacon and pepper. Toss the rice mixture with spinach. Garnish with almonds.

LEMON VEGETABLE ASPIC

1 (3-ounce) package lemon
   gelatin

1 cup boiling water

¾ cup cold water

1 tablespoon white wine vinegar

1 tablespoon lemon juice

⅛ teaspoon salt

1 teaspoon horseradish

½ cup grated carrot

¼ cup sliced radishes

⅓ cup chopped celery

¼ cup chopped green onions

⅓ cup sliced stuffed green olives

½ cup coarsely chopped pecans
   or walnuts (optional)

Lettuce leaves

CREAMY DILL DRESSING

½ cup mayonnaise

½ cup sour cream

1½ teaspoons lemon juice

½ teaspoon dill weed

2 tablespoons chopped parsley

⅛ teaspoon black pepper

1½ teaspoons horseradish

Serves 6-8.

Dissolve lemon gelatin in boiling water. Add cold water, vinegar, lemon juice, salt and horseradish. Mix well. Cool until slightly thickened. Add vegetables and mix. Chill in mold until firm. Unmold and serve on lettuce leaves. Top aspic with a spoonful of Creamy Dill Dressing.

Vegetable substitutes for salad include chopped avocado, diced cucumber and water-packed artichoke hearts (quartered).

To prepare Creamy Dill Dressing, blend dressing ingredients together lightly and refrigerate until serving time. (Makes 1 cup.)

TART ASPARAGUS SALAD

A sophisticated molded salad

2 tablespoons unflavored gelatin

½ cup cold water

½ cup white vinegar

¾ cup sugar

1 cup water

1 tablespoon minced onion

1 teaspoon salt

2 tablespoons lemon juice

1½ cups fresh asparagus (or 10-ounce can of cut green asparagus, drained)

1 (5-ounce) can sliced water chestnuts, drained

1 cup chopped celery

1 (4-ounce) can pimiento, drained

Lettuce

TOPPING

3 tablespoons mayonnaise

1 tablespoon sour cream

¾ teaspoon lemon juice

Serves 8-9.

Dissolve gelatin in ½ cup cold water. Bring vinegar, sugar and 1 cup water to a boil. Add gelatin mixture, onion, salt and lemon juice. Stir thoroughly and cool.

Cut fresh asparagus into ½-inch lengths. Steam 2-3 minutes or until tender crisp. Cool under running water.

Pour cooled gelatin mixture into 9 by 9 inch pan. Add asparagus, water chestnuts, celery and pimiento. Stir carefully to distribute vegetables evenly throughout pan. Refrigerate salad until set.

To serve, cut salad in even squares. Place each piece on a bed of lettuce. Garnish with a dollop of topping.

To prepare topping, stir all topping ingredients together.

TANGY TOMATO ASPIC

To make a main-dish salad, top with shrimp or add shrimp to the aspic

1 (3-ounce) package lemon Jell-o

¾ cup boiling water

1 (8-ounce) can tomato sauce

1½ tablespoons vinegar

½ teaspoon salt

Dash of pepper

Dash of onion juice or onion powder

¼ teaspoon Worcestershire sauce

⅛ teaspoon horseradish

½ cup chopped celery

¼ cup sliced green olives

¼ cup sliced green onions

Lettuce leaves

DRESSING

¼ cup mayonnaise

1 teaspoon lemon juice

Serves 6.

Dissolve Jell-o in boiling water. Add tomato sauce and seasonings and mix well. Add celery, olives and onions. Mix carefully. Pour into 8 by 8-inch pan, 1½ quart mold, or individual molds. Refrigerate several hours until set. Cut in squares or unmold and serve on lettuce leaves. Top each serving with a teaspoon of lemon-mayonnaise dressing.

Prepare dressing by combining mayonnaise and lemon juice. Chill.

MOLDED CRANBERRY SALAD

A wonderful holiday salad

1 (6-ounce) package raspberry
    gelatin

¼ cup sugar

2 cups boiling water

1 medium orange, unpeeled, cut
    in chunks

1 cup sliced celery

2 cups fresh cranberries

1 cup crushed pineapple,
    drained (reserve juice)

1 cup reserved pineapple juice

1 tablespoon lemon juice

Lettuce leaves

LEMON MAYONNAISE

¼ cup mayonnaise

1 teaspoon lemon juice

Serves 12.

Dissolve sugar and gelatin in boiling water. Cool to room temperature. Using metal blade, chop orange in food processor. Add celery and cranberries and pulse until finely chopped. Add to cooled gelatin mixture. Combine with remaining ingredients. Put ½ cup of this mixture into each of 12 molds. Chill overnight. Unmold onto lettuce leaf and serve with 1 teaspoon of Lemon Mayonnaise on top.

Cranberry salad may be placed in a 2-quart ring mold if desired.

To prepare Lemon Mayonnaise, blend mayonnaise and lemon juice well and chill.

Summer Breeze Chicken Salad

The orange dressing is light and refreshing

4 cups cooked diced chicken breast

2 cups fresh pineapple chunks, cut in small pieces

1 cup Mandarin oranges, drained

½ small red onion, sliced in thin rings

8 cups mixed greens, torn in bite-sized pieces

8 slices avocado

½ cup caramelized walnuts

Orange Dressing

⅓ cup orange juice concentrate, do not dilute

2½ tablespoons sugar

2 tablespoons red wine vinegar

1 tablespoon lemon juice

¾ teaspoon grated fresh orange peel

½ teaspoon grated fresh lemon peel

¼ teaspoon salt

Dash white pepper

Caramelized Walnuts

½ cup coarsely chopped walnuts

3 tablespoons granulated sugar

Serves 8.

Prepare Orange Dressing. Blend dressing ingredients together in blender or food processor.

Marinate chicken in Orange Dressing in refrigerator for several hours, then drain and save marinade to pour over salad greens.

Keep other ingredients chilled.

To serve, prepare a bed of greens on individual plates or in a large salad bowl. Lay onion rings on greens, scatter pineapple and oranges over greens. Arrange chicken in center of salad. Top with a fresh slice of avocado. Just before serving, drizzle Orange Dressing from marinated chicken over greens and sprinkle with caramelized walnuts.

To prepare caramelized walnuts, melt sugar slowly in a heavy skillet or saucepan. As soon as sugar has melted and is a light golden brown, quickly stir in walnuts coating well with sugar. Turn into greased pie tin. Let cool, then break apart pieces that have stuck together.

HER ROYAL MAJESTY'S CHICKEN SALAD

A traditional favorite at Albertina's

4 cups cooked diced chicken

1 cup diced celery

1 pound seedless grapes, halved

1 (5-ounce) can sliced water chestnuts, drained

1 (11-ounce) can Mandarin oranges, drained

1 (11-ounce) can pineapple tidbits, drained

1 cup slivered almonds, toasted

8 lettuce leaves

Fresh fruits (optional)

DRESSING

1 cup mayonnaise

2 tablespoons lemon juice

1 tablespoon curry powder

1 tablespoon soy sauce

Serves 8.

Prepare dressing by mixing together all dressing ingredients. Refrigerate.

In a large bowl, combine diced chicken, celery, grapes, water chestnuts and half the dressing. Chill at least 2 hours. At serving time, add well-drained Mandarin oranges, pineapple, almonds and remaining dressing. Serve on lettuce leaf and garnish with fresh fruit such as cantaloupe, papaya, kiwi or wedges of lime.

ALBERTINA'S CHICKEN SALAD

A perfect marriage of fruit and chicken

3 cups cooked cubed chicken or
    turkey breast

1 cup thinly sliced celery

1½ cups cantaloupe balls

1 cup halved green or red
    seedless grapes

Lettuce leaves

½ cup slivered almonds

DRESSING

2 tablespoons sugar

1 tablespoon flour

½ teaspoon salt

¼ teaspoon curry powder

½ cup water

¼ cup cider vinegar

1 egg, beaten

1 tablespoon butter

Serves 5-6.

Prepare dressing. Mix together sugar, flour, salt and curry powder in a small saucepan. Add water, cider vinegar and beaten egg. Cook over medium heat, stirring often, until mixture has thickened (about 5-10 minutes). Add butter and cool.

Combine chicken and celery with half of the dressing. Refrigerate several hours or overnight. Before serving, add cantaloupe balls, grapes and rest of the dressing. Serve on lettuce leaves and sprinkle with slivered almonds.

Spinach Almond Salad with Chicken

2 pounds spinach leaves, washed and stemmed

3 cups diced cooked chicken breast

2 cups diced red apples, unpeeled

⅔ cup golden raisins

¼ cup chopped green onions

2 tablespoons toasted sesame seeds

¾ cup toasted slivered almonds, divided

Dressing

2 tablespoons chutney

1 teaspoon curry powder

¼ teaspoon salt

1 teaspoon dry mustard

¼ teaspoon Tabasco

¼ cup white wine vinegar

2 tablespoons sugar

⅔ cup canola oil

Serves 6.

Prepare dressing. Place all dressing ingredients, except oil, in a food processor. Mix well. Slowly pour oil through the feed tube while machine is running. This will emulsify the dressing. Refrigerate until used.

Cut or tear the spinach leaves into large bite-sized pieces. Refrigerate.

Combine diced chicken, apple, raisins and green onions with ⅔ cup of the dressing. Mix well and chill.

At serving time, add remaining dressing to spinach. Toss lightly and place on individual serving plates. Sprinkle sesame seeds over greens.

Add ½ cup almonds to chicken mixture. Spoon chicken mixture on top of greens and sprinkle remaining almonds on top.

TURKEY CRANBERRY SALAD

Extraordinary!

½ cup dried cranberries

½ cup orange juice, warmed

4 cups cooked diced turkey breast (¾-inch chunks)

1½ cups sliced water chestnuts

1½ cups thinly sliced celery

¾ cup golden raisins

¾ cup coarsely chopped walnuts

8 lettuce leaves

Orange twists and parsley (optional)

CREAM CHEESE DRESSING

3 ounces cream cheese

2 tablespoons cider vinegar

2 tablespoons sugar

⅛ teaspoon garlic salt

¼ teaspoon salt

⅛ teaspoon white pepper

1 tablespoon prepared mustard

2 tablespoons salad oil

2 tablespoons milk

CRANBERRY ORANGE RELISH

½ medium orange

1 cup canned cranberry sauce (whole berries)

Serves 8.

Prepare Cream Cheese Dressing. Mix all dressing ingredients in a food processor until well·blended. Refrigerate. If dressing is too thick to mix well when adding to turkey salad, thin with 1-2 tablespoons more milk.

Pour warmed orange juice over dried cranberries. Cover and let sit for 1-2 hours. Drain cranberries before using.

In a large mixing bowl, combine turkey, cranberries, water chestnuts, celery and raisins. Add the Cream Cheese Dressing and mix well. Cover and refrigerate.

At serving time, set aside ¼ cup of walnuts (for garnish) and stir remaining nuts into the salad. Serve on a lettuce leaf and sprinkle remaining walnuts on top. Garnish with orange twist and parsley sprig. Serve with Cranberry Orange Relish.

To prepare Cranberry Orange Relish. Cut orange half into 4 pieces, do not peel. Place in food processor and pulse until orange is finely chopped, with no large pieces of rind. Add cranberry sauce and blend well. Serve in small individual cups or pass in a relish dish.

CURRIED TURKEY RICE SALAD

Fresh lime is a must

1½ pounds cooked turkey
   breast, cut into ½-inch cubes

3 cups cooked rice

1 large tomato, seeded and
   diced

¾ cup diagonally sliced celery

¾ cup golden raisins

¼ cup chopped peanuts

Lettuce leaves

Tomato wedges

DRESSING

⅔ cup mayonnaise

¼ cup salad oil

¼ cup fresh lime juice

2 teaspoons curry powder

1 teaspoon dill weed

1½ teaspoons dry mustard

1½ teaspoons onion powder

½ teaspoon Tabasco

Serves 8.

Prepare dressing. Slowly add oil and lime juice to mayonnaise. Mix well. Add seasonings and mix. Refrigerate several hours or overnight to develop the flavor.

Combine turkey breast with rice, tomatoes, celery and raisins. Add dressing and mix well. Serve on bed of lettuce and sprinkle chopped nuts on top. Garnish with tomato wedges.

Wild Rice and Turkey Salad

3½ cups cooked long-grain
   white rice

1 cup cooked wild rice

3 cups cooked diced turkey or
   chicken breast

¼ cup diced red bell pepper

¼ cup diced green or yellow
   bell pepper

½ cup finely sliced green onions

Lettuce leaves

½ cup toasted slivered almonds

Apple slices

Tarragon Dressing

1 cup mayonnaise

½ cup tarragon vinegar

¼ teaspoon salt

¼ teaspoon pepper

Serves 8.

Prepare Tarragon Dressing. Place mayonnaise in a small bowl and slowly add tarragon vinegar, stirring well. Mix in salt and pepper.

Combine rices, turkey, bell peppers, green onions and dressing. Mix well. Refrigerate until serving time.

To serve, place lettuce leaves in a large serving bowl or on individual plates. Fill with salad. Sprinkle almonds on top and garnish with unpeeled apple slices.

NOTE: In place of tarragon vinegar, ½ cup mild white vinegar or seasoned rice vinegar, mixed with 2 tablespoons chopped fresh tarragon, (or 2 teaspoons dried) may be substituted.

Chicken Wild Rice Salad with Orange Vinaigrette

An exotic blend

4 cups chicken broth

1 cup wild rice, uncooked

1 cup long-grain brown rice, uncooked

4 chicken breast halves, cooked and cubed

3 green onions, sliced

½ cup golden raisins

½ cup chopped celery

2 teaspoons grated orange rind

1 cup pecans, toasted

Lettuce leaves

2 tablespoons fresh minced chives

Orange Vinaigrette Dressing

¼ cup rice wine vinegar

¼ cup orange juice, freshly squeezed

2 tablespoons Dijon mustard

2 tablespoons mango chutney

½ teaspoon salt

¼ teaspoon white pepper

½ cup canola or vegetable oil

Serves 8-10.

In a large saucepan, bring chicken broth to a boil. Stir in wild rice and simmer covered for 10 minutes. Add brown rice and simmer mixture, covered, until liquid is absorbed (about 30-35 minutes). Remove from heat, uncover and cool to room temperature.

Prepare Orange Vinaigrette Dressing. Combine vinegar, orange juice, mustard, chutney, salt and pepper in a food processor. Blend well. Add oil in a slow steady stream while machine is running. Refrigerate until needed.

In a large bowl, combine rice, chicken, green onions, raisins, celery and grated orange rind. Add dressing and toss gently to mix. Refrigerate.

About a half hour before serving, bring salad out of the refrigerator to take chill off of rice. Add pecans and mix well. Serve on individual lettuce-lined plates or in a large serving bowl. Sprinkle with fresh minced chives.

...LAD WITH CHUTNEY

2 cups cooked diced chicken or turkey

1 cup diced celery

½ cup sliced water chestnuts

¼ cup sliced green onions

1 cup pineapple chunks, drained

½ cup toasted sliced almonds

Green-leaf lettuce

Mandarin oranges

Limes

CHUTNEY DRESSING

½ cup sour cream

3 tablespoons chopped or blended chutney

1 teaspoon grated orange rind

1 teaspoon lemon juice

½ teaspoon curry powder

2 shakes Tabasco

Serves 4.

Prepare Chutney Dressing by combining all dressing ingredients and mixing well. Chill.

Combine chicken or turkey, celery, water chestnuts and green onions with dressing. Just before serving, stir in pineapple and almonds. Serve on green-leaf lettuce. Garnish with Mandarin oranges and slices of fresh lime.

Empress Chicken Salad

3 cups cooked small pasta shells, rinsed (1½ cups uncooked)

½ cup sliced green onions

3 cups thinly sliced, cooked chicken breasts

½ cup sliced celery

½ cup sliced water chestnuts

¼ pound peapods (fresh or frozen)

8 cups fresh spinach leaves

1 cup sliced mushrooms (optional)

¾ cup canned Mandarin oranges, drained

¼ cup toasted sesame seeds

Dressing

1½ teaspoons fresh peeled sliced ginger root

⅓ cup white wine vinegar

⅓ cup soy sauce

2 tablespoons brown sugar

¼ teaspoon black pepper

⅓ cup oil

Serves 8-10.

Prepare dressing. Combine all ingredients, except oil, in food processor. Mix well. Slowly add oil through feed tube while processor is running. Refrigerate overnight to blend flavors. Strain dressing to remove ginger root before using. Mix dressing well as you are using it.

Combine cooked, rinsed pasta shells with the green onion and one-third of the dressing. Mix well and refrigerate.

Cut thinly sliced chicken breasts into 1-inch lengths. Combine chicken, celery and water chestnuts. Add another third of the dressing, mix and refrigerate.

Wash peapods, remove strings and cut in halves or bite-size pieces. Wash spinach, removing stems. Cut or tear into bite-size pieces.

At serving time, place chicken mixture in a large bowl. Add peapods, mushrooms, Mandarin oranges and pasta mixture. Mix gently. Add remaining dressing to spinach leaves. Toss spinach to coat evenly with dressing. Add spinach to chicken and pasta mixture. Toss gently. Serve in large bowl or on individual chilled plates. Sprinkle with toasted sesame seeds.

IMPERIAL CHICKEN SALAD

Great results for big effort

8 boned and skinned chicken
    breast halves

MARINADE FOR CHICKEN

½ cup dry sherry

1 clove garlic, mashed

½ cup soy sauce

2-inch piece ginger root, sliced
    and mashed

SALAD

1 head Romaine, shredded

1 medium head iceberg lettuce,
    shredded

6 green onions, chopped

Roasted and slivered chicken

¼ cup toasted sesame seeds

½ cup toasted almonds,
    chopped or sliced

DRESSING

½ cup salad oil

2 tablespoons lemon juice

2 teaspoons soy sauce

1 teaspoon sesame oil

2 teaspoons dry mustard

3 tablespoons sugar

2 tablespoons white wine vinegar

1 teaspoon grated fresh ginger

1 clove garlic, mashed

WON TONS

3 ounces won ton wrappers

½ cup oil

Serves 10.

Preheat oven to 350 degrees.

To prepare marinade, combine sherry, garlic, soy sauce and ginger. Pour over chicken. Marinate in the refrigerator for several hours or overnight.

Place chicken in a shallow baking pan, removing any ginger root clinging to it. Roast for 20-25 minutes. Cool. Sliver or cube chicken and refrigerate.

Prepare dressing. Combine dressing ingredients and refrigerate. Before using, strain out ginger and garlic.

To prepare salad, place greens and onions in a large bowl. Toss with dressing. Sprinkle with sesame seeds.

Place greens on individual plates and top with chicken. Sprinkle almonds on chicken and arrange won ton strips around the edges. (Crisp chow mein noodles may be substituted for won tons.)

To prepare won tons, cut them in ¾ inch strips. Fry strips in hot oil, one layer at a time, until crisp. Drain on paper towels.

MEDITERRANEAN CHICKEN SALAD

Out of the ordinary

3 cups cubed, cooked chicken breasts

2 medium cucumbers, peeled, seeded and chopped (about 2½ cups)

1 cup (4 ounces) crumbled feta cheese

⅔ cup sliced black olives

Lettuce leaves

Broccoli florets

Tomato wedges

Parsley

AIOLI DRESSING

1 cup mayonnaise

½ cup plain yogurt

1 tablespoon oregano, crushed

2 cloves garlic, finely minced

Serves 5-6.

Prepare Aioli Dressing. Combine all dressing ingredients. Stir. Refrigerate for several hours or overnight.

In a large bowl, combine chicken, cucumber, feta cheese and olives. Add dressing and gently toss mixture until lightly coated. Cover and chill.

Serve on lettuce leaves. Surround with tomato wedges and broccoli florets. Sprinkle fresh chopped parsley on top.

Monterey Chicken Salad

South of the border flavors!

1 large head Romaine lettuce

½ small red onion, sliced

½ cup sliced jicama strips

¼ cup chopped cilantro or parsley

3 cups cooked, diced chicken breasts

2 large tomatoes, seeded and diced

1 (4-ounce) can diced green chiles, drained

3 tablespoons sliced green onions

1 ripe avocado, cubed

¾ cup grated Monterey Jack cheese (3 ounces)

2 ounces (½ can) sliced black olives

Tortilla chips, crushed or broken

Dressing

¾ cup sour cream

¾ cup mayonnaise

1½ - 2 teaspoons cumin

¼ - ½ teaspoon chili powder

⅛ teaspoon Tabasco

1 tablespoon lemon juice

Serves 6.

Combine dressing ingredients. Mix well and refrigerate.

Clean, dry and cut Romaine in 1-inch by 2-inch pieces. Add red onion, jicama and cilantro or parsley. Cover and refrigerate.

In a large bowl, combine chicken, tomatoes, chiles and green onions. Reserve some tomatoes for garnish. Add half the dressing to this mixture. Refrigerate.

Just before serving, dice avocado in ¾-inch cubes and gently fold into chicken mixture.

Toss greens with remainder of dressing.

To serve, place a bed of greens on a platter or individual plates. Arrange chicken mixture on top. Sprinkle chicken with cheese. Garnish with olives and reserved tomatoes. Add crushed tortilla chips around the edges.

CHICKEN SALAD WITH BASIL CREAM

6 whole chicken breasts, boned
   and skinned

3 cups artichoke hearts, diced

5 cups broccoli florets

½ cup olive oil

⅓ cup lemon juice

Large lettuce leaves

3 tomatoes, cut in wedges

1 cup crumbled feta cheese

½ cup chopped parsley

12 whole black olives

BASIL CREAM

1 cup mayonnaise

1 tablespoon pesto

1½ teaspoons lemon juice

¼ teaspoon dry mustard

1 clove garlic, finely minced

1 teaspoon dried basil

Serves 10-12.

Make Basil Cream the day ahead and refrigerate overnight.

Poach chicken breasts in salted water. Simmer over medium-low heat for 20 minutes, or until chicken is no longer pink in center. (Test with sharp knife.) Cool and dice chicken. Combine diced chicken, artichoke hearts and Basil Cream. Mix gently and refrigerate.

Marinate broccoli florets in olive oil and lemon juice for 1-2 hours, stirring occasionally.

At serving time, drain broccoli well and add 3 cups to chicken mixture. Combine gently. Line plates with lettuce leaves. Mound ¾-1 cup chicken salad on each plate. Arrange remaining broccoli florets and tomato wedges around edge. Sprinkle the mound of chicken salad with a tablespoon of feta cheese, add some chopped parsley and top with a whole olive.

To prepare Basil Cream, combine all cream ingredients by stirring together in a small mixing bowl. Refrigerate overnight . If you do not have pesto on hand, add more garlic and basil.

Chicken Broccoli Salad

Don't pass up this one

3 cups cooked chicken

3 cups broccoli florets

2 tablespoons chopped red onion

4 large mushrooms, sliced

Lettuce leaves

Toasted slivered almonds

Dressing

2 tablespoons cider vinegar

3 ounces cream cheese

2 tablespoons sugar

⅛ teaspoon garlic salt

¼ teaspoon salt

1 tablespoon prepared mustard

2 tablespoons milk

2 tablespoons salad oil

Serves 6.

Cut chicken into large bite-sized pieces.

Steam broccoli 2 minutes until bright green color develops. Plunge immediately into ice water to cool. Drain well.

Prepare dressing. Mix all dressing ingredients in a blender or food processor. Refrigerate. At serving time, if dressing is too thick, add a little more milk.

Lightly mix chicken, broccoli, onion and mushrooms. Add part of the dressing and refrigerate. Add more dressing at serving time, as needed. Serve on lettuce leaves. Garnish with almonds.

HEARTY PASTA SALAD WITH PESTO

The combination of feta and pesto make this unique

1 quart cooked tricolor pasta shells (2 cups uncooked)

2 cups julienned Italian salami

¼ cup chopped green onions

½ cup sliced red bell pepper strips

Salt

Pepper, freshly ground

Large lettuce leaves (optional)

½ cup crumbled feta cheese

½ cup sliced Greek or black olives

12 tomato wedges

VINAIGRETTE DRESSING

2 tablespoons red wine vinegar

2 tablespoons crumbled feta cheese

½ cup olive oil

⅓ cup pesto

Serves 6.

Prepare Vinaigrette Dressing. Place red wine vinegar and feta cheese in a food processor or blender. Pulse together. Add olive oil and blend well. Add pesto and barely blend.

In a large bowl, combine cooked shells, salami, green onions, red pepper strips and ½ to ¾ of dressing. Sprinkle with salt and pepper. Mix well and refrigerate.

At serving time, taste and add more salt, pepper and dressing, if needed. Serve in a large bowl or on individual chilled plates lined with lettuce leaves. Sprinkle with crumbled feta cheese and sliced olives. Garnish with tomato wedges.

POLYNESIAN SHRIMP SALAD

Light and breezy like the islands

4 cups cooked spiral pasta

¾ cup sliced water chestnuts

⅓ cup finely diced green pepper

1½ cups pineapple tidbits, well drained

¾ cup Mandarin oranges, drained

½ pound cooked shrimp (cocktail size or larger)

8 large lettuce leaves

⅓ cup cashew nuts

Parsley sprigs

PINEAPPLE CURRY DRESSING

1 cup pineapple juice

1 tablespoon cornstarch

¾ teaspoon curry powder

½ teaspoon salt

1 tablespoon lemon juice

½ cup mayonnaise

½ cup sour cream

Serves 6.

Prepare Pineapple Curry Dressing. Mix cornstarch with 1 tablespoon cold pineapple juice. Combine rest of pineapple juice, cornstarch mixture, curry and salt in small saucepan or double boiler. Cook over medium heat, stirring often, until mixture is hot and thickened. Remove from heat and stir in lemon juice. Cool to room temperature. Combine mayonnaise and sour cream. Slowly pour in cooled pineapple mixture. Blend well. Refrigerate until needed.

Combine pasta, water chestnuts and green pepper with ⅔ of the dressing. Mix well and chill.

At serving time, add pineapple, Mandarin oranges and shrimp. Combine carefully. Add more dressing if needed.

Serve on lettuce leaves. Sprinkle with cashews and garnish with parsley sprigs.

Herbed Rice and Bay Shrimp Salad

Add a chicken salad and fruit for a delightful salad trio

4 cups cooked rice, cooled

½ cup coarsely chopped red bell pepper

½ cup sliced green onions

½ pound bay shrimp

Lettuce

Tomato wedges

Parsley sprigs

Dressing

½ cup mayonnaise

¼ cup olive oil

2 tablespoons white wine vinegar

1 tablespoon dried dill weed

¼ teaspoon salt

¼ teaspoon pepper

Serves 6.

Prepare dressing. Measure mayonnaise into a small bowl. Slowly add olive oil and white wine vinegar, mixing well. Add dill, salt and pepper.

Add dressing to cooked rice. Mix well. Add red peppers and green onions and mix again. Refrigerate overnight.

At serving time, add shrimp to rice mixture and combine gently. Serve on lettuce. Garnish with extra shrimp, tomato wedges and parsley sprigs.

ARTICHOKE AND SHRIMP SALAD

1 cup uncooked long-grain rice

2½ cups chicken broth

⅓ cup diced green peppers

¼ cup sliced green onions

½ cup sliced pimiento-stuffed olives

¼ cup chopped fresh parsley

1 cup marinated artichoke hearts, drained (save the liquid)

½ pound shrimp meat

Lettuce leaves

Cherry tomatoes halved

Parsley

Green pepper rings

DRESSING

¾ cup mayonnaise

1½ teaspoons cider vinegar

¾ teaspoon curry powder

6 tablespoons liquid from marinated artichokes

⅛ teaspoon Tabasco

Serves 5-6.

Combine and mix all dressing ingredients. Refrigerate.

Cook rice in chicken broth in a covered saucepan 20 minutes or until all liquid is absorbed. Cool rice to room temperature. Add dressing and refrigerate, uncovered, until rice is chilled.

To rice mixture, add peppers, onions, olives, parsley and drained artichokes. Cover and refrigerate several hours or overnight.

Just before serving, add shrimp. Serve on lettuce leaves and garnish with halved cherry tomatoes and parsley sprigs, topping with sliced green pepper rings.

SHRIMP AND PEA SALAD

Also good as a first-course salad

1 pound petite frozen peas,
   thawed and drained

1 cup cooked shrimp, drained

1 cup diced celery

¼ cup chopped red onion

½ cup chopped cashews

Lettuce leaves

DRESSING

½ cup sour cream or yogurt

3 tablespoons mayonnaise

¼ teaspoon salt

¼ teaspoon black pepper

1 tablespoon lemon juice

1 teaspoon dill weed

¼ teaspoon horseradish

Serves 4-6.

Combine peas, shrimp, celery and onion. Combine dressing ingredients, blending until smooth. Mix dressing into salad. Chill. Just before serving, fold in cashew nuts. Serve on crisp lettuce.

Greek Salad with Orzo and Shrimp

If you haven't tried orzo, this is a great way to start

1 ⅓ cups uncooked orzo (rice-shaped pasta)

¼ cup finely sliced green onions

1 large tomato, seeded and diced

2 ounces sliced black olives

3 ounces crumbled feta cheese

½ pound cooked bay shrimp

Leafy lettuce

Tomato wedges

Parsley or fresh baby dill

Dressing

3 tablespoons fresh lemon juice

1 ½ tablespoons red wine vinegar

1 ½ cloves garlic, minced

¼ teaspoon salt

⅛ teaspoon black pepper

1 ½ teaspoons dry dill weed

3 tablespoons olive oil

Serves 6.

Combine all dressing ingredients. Mix well.

Cook orzo in salted water according to package directions. Rinse in cold water and drain well. Add dressing, green onions, tomatoes, olives and feta cheese. Do not worry if the salad looks oily; orzo will absorb the extra dressing as it cools. Refrigerate several hours or overnight.

At serving time, add bay shrimp. Taste and add more dill weed, if needed. Serve on leafy lettuce and garnish with tomato wedges and parsley sprigs or fresh baby dill.

ALBERTINA'S SPECIAL DRESSING

Delicious served over mixed greens

1 ¼ cups mayonnaise

½ cup salad oil

¼ cup honey

¼ cup prepared mustard

3 tablespoons fresh lemon juice

1 teaspoon celery seed

¼ teaspoon dry mustard

¼ teaspoon curry powder

2 green onions, finely chopped

1 tablespoon finely chopped
   fresh parsley

Makes 2 cups.

Place mayonnaise in mixing bowl. Set aside. Combine oil, honey, prepared mustard, lemon juice, celery seed, dry mustard and curry powder in a food processor. Blend well. Gradually stir blended ingredients into mayonnaise. Mix by hand. Stir in onions and parsley. Chill.

CELERY SEED DRESSING

Wonderful dressing for greens with melons and/or citrus fruits

¼ cup cider vinegar

½ cup sugar

1 teaspoon salt

1 teaspoon celery seed

¼ teaspoon paprika

¾ teaspoon onion salt

1 cup salad oil

Makes 1 ½ cups.

Combine all ingredients except oil in a food processor. Blend well. Slowly add oil while machine is running. Store in refrigerator.

CREAMY DILL DRESSING

Good on greens and great on salmon

½ cup mayonnaise

½ cup plain yogurt

¼ cup sour cream

½ cup buttermilk

1 tablespoon dill weed

¼ teaspoon onion powder

¼ teaspoon black pepper

Parmesan cheese, optional

Makes 1¾ cups.

Put mayonnaise in mixing bowl. Add yogurt and sour cream. Mix well. Slowly add buttermilk. Stir well. Add dill weed, onion powder and pepper.

Pour over greens and toss. Sprinkle Parmesan cheese over top of each serving.

CREAMY FRUIT DRESSING

Serve a dollop of dressing on a fresh fruit cup or on an arranged fruit salad for a refreshing treat

1 cup sour cream

½ cup powdered sugar*

1 teaspoon fresh lemon juice

1 teaspoon fresh grated lemon rind

Makes 1 cup.

Combine all ingredients in a bowl. Stir together. Do not use a food processor.

Store covered in refrigerator.

*Less sugar may be used if you prefer a more tart dressing.

CREAMY MUSTARD DRESSING

Albertina's serves this dressing over asparagus

1 cup mayonnaise

¼ cup Dijon mustard

½ cup sour cream

¼ cup white wine vinegar

2 tablespoons sugar

1 teaspoon dry dill weed

¼ teaspoon salt

¼ teaspoon white pepper

Makes 2½ cups.

Mix all ingredients together by hand or use an electric mixer. Refrigerate 2-4 hours to blend flavors.

Place asparagus on bed of greens. Drizzle dressing over asparagus and greens. Garnish with pimiento.

HONEY MUSTARD DRESSING

Tangy!

⅓ cup honey

¼ cup Dijon mustard

1 clove garlic, minced

2 tablespoons fresh lemon juice

¼ cup seasoned rice vinegar

1 cup canola oil

Makes 2 cups.

In a blender or food processor, combine honey, mustard, garlic, lemon juice and vinegar. Process until well mixed, about 1 minute.

With motor running, add canola oil in a slow, steady stream, processing until dressing has a smooth and creamy texture.

Store covered in refrigerator.

Lady Albertina's Bleu Cheese Dressing

This dressing is perfect over endive or other greens, garnished with croutons and mushroom or avocado slices

2 cloves garlic

2 tablespoons minced green onion

1 tablespoon lemon juice

½ teaspoon salt

⅛ teaspoon black pepper

1 cup mayonnaise

½ cup sour cream

¼ cup crumbled bleu cheese

¼ cup minced parsley

Makes 2 cups.

In a food processor, chop garlic and onion. Add lemon juice, salt, pepper, mayonnaise and sour cream. Mix well. Add bleu cheese and blend. Add parsley and mix. Refrigerate.

Orange Dressing

Excellent dressing for greens topped with fruit such as oranges, melons and grapefruit

1½ tablespoons orange juice concentrate (not diluted)

1½ tablespoons water

1½ tablespoons lemon juice

Grated rind of ½ orange

¼ cup powdered sugar

½ teaspoon paprika

¼ teaspoon salt

¼ teaspoon dry mustard

¼ cup salad oil

Makes ½ cup.

Place all ingredients except oil in food processor. Mix until well blended. With motor running, add oil in a slow, steady stream, mixing well.

Store covered in refrigerator.

POPPY SEED DRESSING

A perfect dressing for greens with strawberries

1 cup sugar

2 teaspoons dry mustard

2 teaspoons salt

⅔ cup white wine vinegar

¼ cup chopped onion*

2 cups salad oil

1½ tablespoons poppy seeds

Makes 3½ cups.

Blend sugar, mustard, salt, vinegar and onion in blender or food processor. With motor running, add oil slowly. Stir in poppy seeds. Refrigerate.

Serve over greens with fruit.

*For a pretty pink color, use red onions.

SALVATORE'S SALAD DRESSING

Superb with Italian dishes

2 tablespoons minced onion

2 teaspoons salt

¾ teaspoon Worcestershire sauce

¾ teaspoon dry mustard

¾ teaspoon basil

¾ teaspoon oregano

¾ teaspoon sugar

¾ teaspoon pepper

¼ cup red wine vinegar

1 tablespoon lemon juice

½ cup olive oil

Makes 1 cup.

Blend all ingredients, except olive oil, in food processor. Slowly add olive oil while processor is running. Refrigerate.

Serve over tossed green salads.

SWEET AND SOUR DRESSING

A great compatible partner for a spinach salad with water chestnuts, cooked bacon bits and hard-cooked eggs

⅓ cup vinegar

½ cup sugar

¼ cup catsup

2 teaspoons Worcestershire sauce

¼ medium onion, cut in chunks

1 cup salad oil

Makes 2 cups.

Place all ingredients, except oil, in blender or food processor and mix well. Slowly add oil while processor is running. Refrigerate.

SWEET AND SOUR CURRY DRESSING

⅔ cup sugar

½ cup red wine vinegar

3 tablespoons lemon juice

2 shakes of Tabasco

4 tablespoons chili sauce

1 tablespoon Worcestershire sauce

½ teaspoon dry mustard

¼ teaspoon curry powder

1 large garlic clove, minced

½ cup oil

Makes 1¾ cups.

Combine all ingredients except oil in food processor. Blend well. Slowly add oil while processor is running. Refrigerate.

This dressing is used in the sauce for Chicken a l'Orange.

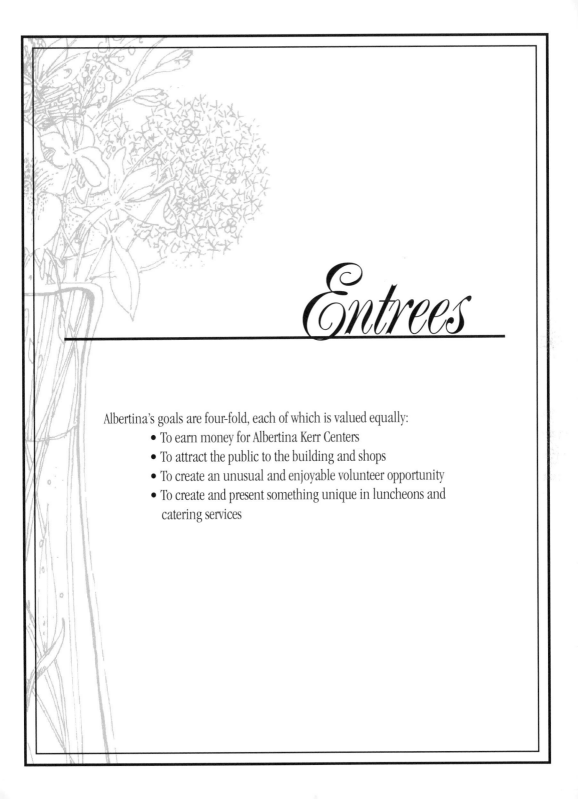

Entrees

Albertina's goals are four-fold, each of which is valued equally:

- To earn money for Albertina Kerr Centers
- To attract the public to the building and shops
- To create an unusual and enjoyable volunteer opportunity
- To create and present something unique in luncheons and catering services

CHICKEN SALTIMBOCCA

½ cup dry bread crumbs

2 tablespoons grated Parmesan cheese

⅛ teaspoon sage

2 tablespoons fresh parsley or 1 tablespoon dry flakes

1 tablespoon margarine, melted

6 (4-ounce) chicken breast halves, boned and skinned

6 thin slices of ham, same size as chicken breast

1¼ cups grated Swiss cheese

6 tomato slices, ¼ inch thick

¼ cup chicken broth

¼ cup white wine

Orzo or rice

Serves 6.

Preheat oven to 350 degrees.

Combine bread crumbs, Parmesan cheese, sage and parsley. Pour melted margarine over mixture and stir well. Set aside.

Lay chicken breasts in greased baking pan. Top each breast with 1 slice of ham. Sprinkle a scant ¼ cup of Swiss cheese evenly over each serving. Lay 1 tomato slice over cheese in center of each breast. Sprinkle bread-crumb mixture over tomato and chicken. Combine broth and wine. Pour mixture between chicken breasts. Bake, uncovered, for 30 minutes or until done. Serve with orzo or rice.

CRANBERRY GLAZED CHICKEN

The color makes this a festive entrée for the holidays

½ cup chopped onion

1 tablespoon butter

⅓ cup catsup

⅓ cup cranberry juice

⅓ cup brown sugar

1 tablespoon cider vinegar

2 teaspoons dry mustard

6 (4-ounce) chicken breast halves, boned and skinned

1¼ cups fresh or frozen cranberries, rinsed

Serves 6.

Preheat oven to 350 degrees.

Sauté onion in butter until translucent and slightly golden. Add catsup, cranberry juice, brown sugar, vinegar and mustard. Heat sauce for 10-15 minutes on low heat to blend flavors.

Place chicken breasts in a greased baking dish. Spoon half of the sauce over chicken breasts. Add cranberries to remaining sauce and set aside. Bake chicken for 15 minutes. Remove from oven. Spoon remaining sauce over chicken. Bake another 10-15 minutes until chicken is done. Serve with parsleyed rice.

CHICKEN DIVAN

A traditional dish at Albertina's

3 cups cooked chicken, cubed

3 cups broccoli florets, lightly steamed and drained

2 (10-ounce) cans cream of chicken soup

1 cup mayonnaise

1 teaspoon lemon juice

2 tablespoons sherry

½ teaspoon curry powder

½ cup Parmesan cheese

½ cup buttered bread crumbs

Serves 6.

Preheat oven to 350 degrees.

Arrange chicken in the bottom of a greased 7 by 11-inch casserole. Place broccoli on top of chicken. Combine next 6 ingredients and spoon over broccoli. Cover with bread crumbs. Bake uncovered for 35-40 minutes.

CHICKEN ZORBA

A robust combination of flavors that may be prepared the day before.
Serve with wild or white rice and CARDAMOM CARROTS.

8 (4-ounce) chicken breast
   halves, boned and skinned

⅔ cup dried apricots

½ cup dry white wine

¼ cup brown sugar, divided

¼ cup olive oil

¼ cup red wine vinegar

¼ cup green olives, pitted and
   cut in fourths

¼ cup capers, drained

1½ tablespoons dried oregano

¼ teaspoon freshly ground
   pepper

¼ teaspoon salt

⅛ teaspoon crushed red pepper

2 medium-sized bay leaves

1 small garlic head, minced

1 tablespoon chopped cilantro

Cooked hot rice

Serves 8.

In a Pyrex pan, arrange the chicken breasts in 1 layer. Combine the remaining ingredients, except 2 tablespoons of brown sugar and the cilantro. Pour this mixture over the chicken so that the apricots, olives, capers and bay leaves are evenly distributed. Cover and refrigerate overnight.

Preheat oven to 350 degrees.

Sprinkle the remaining 2 tablespoons of brown sugar over the chicken. Bake uncovered for about 30 minutes, or until done, basting often.

To serve, arrange a chicken half on a bed of rice and spoon sauce over all. Sprinkle with cilantro.

APRICOT CHICKEN DIVINE

This is divine

6 (4-ounce) chicken breast
   halves, boned and skinned

1 tablespoon margarine

1 tablespoon olive oil

½ cup flour

1 teaspoon salt

½ cup apricot preserves

1 tablespoon Dijon mustard

½ cup plain nonfat yogurt

3 tablespoons slivered almonds

Cooked hot rice

Serves 6.

Preheat oven to 350 degrees.

Melt margarine and olive oil in baking dish. Shake chicken pieces in bag with flour and salt. Shake off excess flour and place chicken in a single layer in baking dish. Combine apricot preserves, mustard and yogurt. Spread mixture over chicken pieces. Bake 25-30 minutes or until done. Sprinkle slivered almonds over chicken pieces for last 10-15 minutes of baking. Serve with parsleyed rice or a mixture of white and wild rice.

CREAMY CHICKEN ENCHILADAS

An easy crowd pleaser

2 cups sour cream

1 (7-ounce) can diced green
   chiles

3 (10-ounce) cans cream of
   chicken soup

4 cups cooked, finely diced
   chicken breasts

¾ cup chopped green onions

12 (8-inch) flour tortillas

1½ cups grated cheddar cheese

Serves 8-12.

Preheat oven to 350 degrees.

Mix sour cream, chiles and chicken soup to make a sauce. Divide sauce in half. To one half, add chicken and onions. Spoon chicken mixture equally onto tortillas. Roll each tortilla and place seam side down in a greased 9 by 13-inch casserole. Cover with remaining sauce and sprinkle with cheese. Bake for 20-30 minutes or until hot and bubbly.

Chicken Oriental in a Spinach Nest

This tasty hot sauce "cooks" the spinach

½ pound raw fresh spinach,
    cleaned and dried

6 large chicken breast halves,
    skinned and boned

¼ cup cornstarch

2 tablespoons butter

2 tablespoons oil

1 slice fresh ginger

Oriental Sauce

1 cup chicken broth

⅓ cup sugar

⅓ cup fresh lemon juice

2 tablespoons water

1 tablespoon dry sherry

1½ tablespoons soy sauce

2 slices fresh ginger

Serves 6.

Prepare Oriental Sauce. Mix all sauce ingredients and heat to a simmer. Keep hot. Discard ginger before serving.

Prepare spinach and place into 6 individual casseroles. Dredge chicken breasts in cornstarch. Heat butter, oil and ginger. Sauté chicken until golden brown on both sides and cooked through. Place a chicken breast on top of spinach in each casserole. Pour hot sauce over chicken breasts and spinach. This sauce heats the spinach so that it appears cooked.

CHICKEN ARTICHOKE PUFFS

Very Southwest

1 package (10 ounces) frozen
   puff pastry shells

2 cups cooked chicken, cut into
   small cubes

1 cup grated Monterey Jack
   cheese

1 jar (6½ ounces) marinated
   artichoke hearts, drained and
   quartered

½ cup sour cream

1 can (4 ounces) chopped green
   chiles

½ teaspoon chili powder

2 green onions, chopped

1 clove garlic, minced

1 tablespoon lemon juice

¼ teaspoon salt

1 egg

1 tablespoon milk

Serves 6.

Separate pastry shells and set aside to defrost for 30 minutes.

Preheat oven to 400 degrees.

Combine chicken, cheese, artichoke hearts, sour cream, chiles, chili powder, onions, garlic, lemon and salt. Mix thoroughly.

Roll each pastry shell into an 8-inch circle. Place a rounded ½ cup of chicken mixture in the center of each circle. Lightly moisten edges of pastry. Close pastry circle over the top of chicken, overlap and pinch to seal. Roll up ends and pinch making certain that all edges are sealed. Place seam side down on ungreased baking sheet, allowing plenty of space between pastries. Beat egg and milk together and brush tops of each serving. Poke several holes in each pastry with a fork to allow venting.

Bake for 30 minutes or until puffed and golden. Serve immediately.

POULET D'ARTICHOKE CREPES

A French crepe with an Italian twist

¼ cup butter or margarine

1 cup chopped onion

1 clove garlic, minced

2 cups sliced mushrooms

3 cups cooked cubed chicken or
    turkey

1 (6-ounce) jar marinated
    artichoke hearts, drained and
    chopped

4 cups grated Swiss cheese,
    divided in half

Salt and pepper

16 (8-inch) crepes*

SAUCE

1 (28-ounce) can tomato sauce

1 teaspoon dried basil

1 teaspoon dried oregano

1 (6-ounce) jar marinated
    artichoke hearts, drained and
    chopped

Serves 8.

Preheat oven to 350 degrees.

Melt butter in a large skillet over medium heat. Cook onions and garlic until tender. Add mushrooms and cook until softened (2 or 3 minutes). Remove from heat and cool mixture. Stir in chicken or turkey, artichokes and 2 cups of cheese. Season to taste with salt and pepper. Place crepes on work surface with light-colored side up. Divide turkey or chicken mixture (about ⅓ cup each) equally among crepes and roll up. Arrange crepes in single layer, seam side down, in greased 9 by 13-inch pan. Combine all sauce ingredients. Spoon sauce over prepared crepes and sprinkle with remaining cheese. Bake for 30-35 minutes.

*See BASIC CREPE RECIPE page 131.

Chicken a l'Orange

Delicious served with Lemon Pilaf

8 (4-ounce) chicken breast
   halves, boned and skinned

Salt and pepper

8 half slices of orange with rind

1 cup orange marmalade

Sweet and Sour Curry Dressing

⅓ cup sugar

¼ cup salad oil

¼ cup red wine vinegar

1½ tablespoons lemon juice

2 shakes Tabasco

2 tablespoons chili sauce

1½ teaspoons Worcestershire
   sauce

¼ teaspoon dry mustard

⅛ teaspoon curry powder

1 small clove garlic, minced

Serves 8.

Preheat oven to 350 degrees.

Place chicken breasts in a single layer in greased baking pan. Sprinkle lightly with salt and pepper. Lay a half slice of orange on each breast. Combine orange marmalade and Sweet and Sour Curry Dressing to make sauce. Pour sauce over chicken, coating well. Bake for 30-35 minutes or until done.

To prepare Sweet and Sour Curry Dressing, combine all dressing ingredients and mix well. Mix again just before using. Makes approximately 1 cup.

PIQUANT CHICKEN

A Cinco de Mayo treat

8 (4-ounce) chicken breast halves, skinned and boned

1 (7-ounce) can diced green chiles

¼ pound Monterey Jack cheese, grated

½ cup fine bread crumbs

¼ cup Parmesan cheese, grated

½ teaspoon chili powder

½ teaspoon garlic salt

¼ teaspoon cumin

¼ teaspoon pepper

6 tablespoons butter, melted

SALSA

1 (15-ounce) can tomato sauce

½ teaspoon cumin

⅓ cup sliced green onions

⅛ teaspoon pepper

Dash of Tabasco sauce

Serves 8.

Preheat oven to 350 degrees.

Pound chicken breasts between waxed paper to ¼ inch thickness. Mix chiles and grated Monterey Jack cheese. Divide chile-cheese mixture in 8 portions and spread in the center of each chicken breast. Roll up and tuck ends under. Combine bread crumbs, Parmesan cheese, chili powder, garlic salt, cumin and pepper. Dip each stuffed breast in melted butter and roll in crumb mixture. Place them, seam side down, in a 9 by 13-inch baking pan and drizzle with a little melted butter. Bake, uncovered, for 30-40 minutes. Serve with salsa and steamed rice.

To prepare salsa, combine all salsa ingredients and heat well.

Chicken Parmesan with Caper Sauce

2 tablespoons flour

¼ teaspoon salt

⅛ teaspoon pepper

1 egg

1 tablespoon water

¾ cup bread crumbs

¼ cup parmesan cheese

4 (4-ounce) chicken breast halves, boned and skinned

1 tablespoon butter

1 tablespoon cooking oil

½ cup dry white wine

1 tablespoon capers

1 teaspoon beef base or 1 beef bouillon cube

2 cups cooked rice, hot

Parsley sprigs

Serves 4.

Preheat oven to 350 degrees.

Combine flour, salt and pepper on waxed paper. Beat egg with water. Combine bread crumbs and cheese in a separate pan. Roll chicken in flour mixture, dip in egg and roll in crumb mixture. Heat butter and oil in a frying pan and sauté chicken until browned on each side. Remove chicken to a small baking pan and bake 10-15 minutes or until cooked through. Add white wine, capers and beef base to frying pan, scraping up browned pieces. Cook 1 minute. Place hot cooked rice in individual casseroles. Place chicken on rice. Spoon sauce carefully over chicken so that capers stay on top of chicken. Garnish with parsley.

CHICKEN PESTO IN PUFF PASTRY

Do-ahead elegance

6 chicken breast halves, boned, skinned, poached and cooled

4 tablespoons pesto

6 thin slices Monterey Jack or provolone cheese

6 thin slices cooked ham (4 inches by 6 inches)

1 package frozen puff pastry shells, defrosted

1 egg white, slightly beaten

Parmesan cheese

Poppy or sesame seeds (optional)

Serves 6.

Spread pesto evenly, over each chicken breast half. Layer a slice of cheese and then a slice of ham on top of each breast. Roll each pastry shell into an 8-10 inch circle. Place chicken on each pastry circle and wrap, pinching seam to seal. Place seam side down on ungreased baking sheet; brush with egg white. Sprinkle each with Parmesan cheese and, if desired, poppy or sesame seeds. Refrigerate for at least 30 minutes. Bake in a preheated 400 degree oven for 25-30 minutes or until puffed and golden brown.

NOTE: To poach chicken breasts, cover with salted water or diluted chicken broth. Bring water to a boil. Turn heat down immediately and simmer on low heat for 20 minutes. Remove from water and cool.

CHUTNEY GLAZED CHICKEN

Simplicity with a flare

8 (4-ounce) chicken breast halves, boned and skinned

Salt and pepper

1½ cups orange juice

½ cup raisins

½ cup chutney, pureed

½ teaspoon thyme

2 teaspoons cinnamon

½ teaspoon curry powder

½ cup toasted slivered almonds

Serves 8.

Preheat oven to 350 degrees.

Arrange chicken in a 9 by 13-inch baking dish. Sprinkle with salt and pepper. Combine orange juice, raisins, chutney, thyme, cinnamon and curry powder. Pour over chicken. Bake for 30-35 minutes or until done, basting occasionally. Sprinkle with almonds and serve with rice.

CHICKEN BREASTS WITH ARTICHOKE AND MUSHROOMS

A palate pleaser

8 (4-ounce) chicken breast halves, boned and skinned

3 cups chicken broth

1 (14-ounce) can artichoke hearts

½ pound fresh mushrooms, sliced

SAUCE

4 tablespoons butter

4 tablespoons flour

1 cup reserved chicken broth

¾ cup half and half

⅛ teaspoon pepper

¼ teaspoon salt

½ cup grated Parmesan cheese

¼ cup vermouth or dry white wine

Serves 8.

Preheat oven to 325 degrees.

Simmer chicken breasts in broth for 15 minutes. Reserve 1 cup of broth. Arrange breasts in 9 by 13-inch baking dish. Drain artichoke hearts and distribute over chicken. Distribute mushrooms over chicken. Pour sauce over chicken and bake 20-25 minutes. May be served with rice or pasta.

To prepare sauce, melt butter and stir in flour. Add chicken broth, half and half, salt and pepper and whisk over medium heat until thickened. Add Parmesan cheese and vermouth.

CHICKEN MUSHROOM AU GRATIN

Tarragon is the special flavor of this company dish

2 cups quartered fresh
    mushrooms

½ cup butter, divided

⅓ cup flour

1 ¼ cups chicken broth

⅔ cup half and half

⅓ cup white wine

½ teaspoon salt

⅛ teaspoon cayenne pepper

1 teaspoon dried tarragon

1 tablespoon Dijon mustard

⅓ cup grated Swiss cheese

2 cups diced cooked chicken

3 cups cooked orzo

½ cup Parmesan cheese

Paprika

Serves 7-8.

Preheat oven to 350 degrees.

Sauté mushrooms in 2 tablespoons butter. Drain and set aside.

In a 2-quart saucepan, melt the remaining butter on medium heat. Stir in flour and cook for 2 minutes. Gradually, add chicken broth, half and half and wine, stirring constantly. Add salt, cayenne pepper, tarragon and mustard. Continue to heat and stir until sauce is thickened. Add Swiss cheese, chicken and sautéed mushrooms.

Place cooked orzo in greased individual casseroles or in large casserole dish. Put chicken-mushroom mixture over orzo. Sprinkle with Parmesan cheese and paprika. Bake for 15-20 minutes or until hot and bubbly.

Chicken

½ cup butter

1 clove garlic, minced

5 teaspoons Dijon mustard

1 ½ cups Panko crumbs or
   coarse bread crumbs

⅓ cup grated Parmesan cheese

¼ teaspoon paprika

⅓ cup dried parsley flakes
   (optional)

8 (4-ounce) chicken breast
   halves, boned and skinned

Dijon Sauce

2 tablespoons Dijon mustard

¼ cup mayonnaise

Serves 8.

Make marinade by melting butter in a saucepan. Add garlic and sauté on medium-low heat for 5 minutes. Blend in Dijon mustard, stirring well. Cool enough to touch but not to solidify. Whip vigorously until mixture thickens.

Mix bread crumbs with Parmesan cheese, paprika and parsley to make a breading mixture.

Dip breasts in marinade, then in bread crumb mixture, packing crumbs to coat well.

Place chicken in a greased 9 by 13-inch pan. Can be refrigerated up to several hours at this point.

Preheat oven to 350 degrees.

Bake chicken for 30 minutes or until done. Serve with parsleyed rice. Spoon Dijon Sauce over the top.

To prepare Dijon Sauce, blend mustard and mayonnaise.

CRISPY LEMON CHICKEN

10 (4-ounce) chicken breast
   halves, boned and skinned

½ cup grated Parmesan cheese

1 teaspoon garlic salt

½ teaspoon black pepper

2 cups fresh soft bread crumbs

½ cup melted butter

Paprika

LEMON SAUCE

¾ cup melted butter

6 tablespoons lemon juice

3 cloves garlic

¾ teaspoon lemon pepper
   seasoning

¾ teaspoon salt

Serves 10.

Preheat oven to 350 degrees.

Combine Parmesan cheese, garlic salt and pepper. Add bread crumbs and mix well. Dip each chicken breast in melted butter and then in crumb mixture. Arrange in a shallow greased baking pan. Sprinkle with paprika. Bake for 20 minutes. Remove from oven and spoon Lemon Sauce over each breast, using all the sauce. Return to oven and bake for 5-10 minutes more or until breasts are done. Serve with parsleyed rice.

To prepare Lemon Sauce, combine all sauce ingredients. Simmer for 5-10 minutes on very low heat. Remove garlic.

ALMOND LEMON CHICKEN

Lemon marmalade imparts a special flavor

6 (4-ounce) chicken breast
    halves, skinned and boned

¾ cup lemon juice

¼ cup Dijon mustard

4 cloves garlic, minced

½ teaspoon white pepper

¾ cup olive oil

Paprika

¼ cup toasted sliced almonds

Cooked hot rice

Parsley

SAUCE

¾ cup reserved marinade

1 cup chicken broth

2 tablespoons cornstarch

3 tablespoons cold water

2 tablespoons lemon marmalade
    (or 2 tablespoons orange
    marmalade and 1 tablespoon
    lemon juice)

2 tablespoons butter

¼ teaspoon cayenne pepper

Serves 6.

Make marinade for chicken by combining lemon juice, mustard, garlic, pepper and olive oil. Beat well. Remove ¾ cup marinade and reserve to use in sauce. Add chicken breasts to remaining marinade and refrigerate for 1-2 hours.

Preheat oven to 350 degrees.

Drain chicken, discarding this marinade. Place chicken in 7 by 11-inch greased baking dish. Bake for 15 minutes. Make sauce and pour over chicken. Sprinkle with paprika. Top with toasted almonds. Return chicken to oven and bake another 10-15 minutes or until done. Serve with rice, spooning some hot sauce over rice. Garnish with parsley.

To prepare sauce, combine reserved marinade and chicken broth in a saucepan. Mix cornstarch and water. Stir into liquids and cook over medium heat until thickened, stirring constantly. Add marmalade and stir until melted. Mix in butter and cayenne pepper. Remove from heat.

Hawaiian Chicken

May be topped with toasted sesame seeds and sliced green onion

8 (4-ounce) chicken breast
   halves, skinned and boned

Marinade

2 cups soy sauce

1 cup water

1 cup sugar

¼ teaspoon powdered ginger

3 cloves garlic, minced

¼ cup vermouth

Serves 8.

Combine all marinade ingredients and pour over chicken. Cover and refrigerate at least 2 hours or overnight.

Preheat oven to 350 degrees.

To cook, remove chicken from marinade. Place in baking pan and bake for 20-30 minutes.

CHICKEN FLORENTINE IN PHYLLO

1 cup finely chopped onion

2 tablespoons margarine

1 (10-ounce) package frozen chopped spinach, thawed and squeezed dry

1 pound ricotta cheese

1 egg, slightly beaten

¼ cup Parmesan cheese

1½ teaspoons Italian herbs

⅛ teaspoon salt

⅛ teaspoon pepper

16 sheets phyllo

½ - ¾ cup butter, melted

8 (4-ounce) chicken breasts, boned and skinned

3 tablespoons Parmesan cheese

Paprika

Serves 8.

Preheat oven to 375 degrees.

Sauté onion in margarine until soft. Combine with the next 7 ingredients and mix well. Place 2 sheets of phyllo together. Brush top surface with melted butter. Place a chicken breast about 3 inches from the bottom in the middle of the sheet. Place ⅓ cup spinach mixture on top of the chicken. Fold bottom of phyllo up and over chicken and filling. Fold both sides inward, forming a package enclosing chicken. Roll package to top of phyllo, ending with filling on top and seam side down. Repeat this procedure with each chicken breast. Place in baking dish and brush tops with melted butter. Bake for 20 minutes. Remove from oven and brush tops again with melted butter. Sprinkle with Parmesan cheese and paprika. Return to oven and bake 10 more minutes.

Tarragon Chicken in Phyllo

Impress your guests with this lovely wrapped package

12 (4-ounce) chicken breast
   halves, boned and skinned

Salt and pepper

24 sheets phyllo dough

⅔ cup melted butter

⅓ cup Parmesan cheese, for
   topping

Sauce

1½ cups mayonnaise

1 cup chopped green onion

⅓ cup lemon juice

2 cloves garlic, minced

2 teaspoons dried tarragon

¼ cup sour cream

Serves 12.

Preheat oven to 375 degrees.

Combine ingredients for sauce. Sprinkle chicken breasts with salt and pepper. Place 2 sheets of phyllo on a flat surface and brush with melted butter. Spread 1½ tablespoons of sauce on each side of chicken breast. Place chicken breast about 3 inches from bottom in the center of the phyllo. Fold bottom of phyllo up and over the chicken. Fold both sides of the phyllo inward. Roll loosely to form a package enclosing the chicken. Place on ungreased baking sheet, seam side down. Brush lightly with butter. Bake 15 minutes. Remove from oven, brush with melted butter again and sprinkle with Parmesan cheese. Return to oven and bake 10-15 minutes more or until golden brown.

...POON CHICKEN

...rves this at Christmas time because it is special

8 (4-ounce) chicken breast
  halves, boned and skinned

1 (8-ounce) cream cheese

3 tablespoons fresh chopped
  parsley

2 tablespoons lemon juice

3 tablespoons chopped chives

Salt and pepper

Paprika

3 slices pepper bacon, cut in
  thirds

Cooked hot rice

Serves 8.

Preheat oven to 400 degrees.

Place chicken breasts between waxed paper and pound to ½-inch thickness. Combine softened cream cheese, parsley, lemon juice and chives. Spread thickly on center of underside of chicken breasts. Roll breasts loosely, turn ends under and place in lightly greased baking pan, seam side down. Sprinkle chicken rolls with salt, pepper and paprika. Place a bacon slice over top of each.

Bake for 25-35 minutes until chicken is cooked. If bacon needs crisping, broil 3-5 minutes. Cheese filling melts and forms a sauce for the chicken. Serve with rice and spoon sauce over rice.

SESAME CHICKEN

8 (4-ounce) chicken breast
    halves, skinned and boned

½ cup flour

½ teaspoon salt

¼ teaspoon pepper

1 teaspoon thyme

2 eggs, beaten

3 tablespoons milk

2 cups soft bread crumbs

¼ cup sesame seeds

¼ cup olive oil (may use ⅛ cup
    corn oil and ⅛ cup olive oil)

Serves 8.

Preheat oven to 350 degrees.

Combine the following ingredients, using 3 bowls. First bowl: flour, salt, pepper and thyme. Second bowl: beaten eggs and milk. Third bowl: bread crumbs and sesame seeds.

Dip chicken breasts in flour mixture, then egg mixture and finally in bread crumbs and sesame seeds. Be sure to coat heavily.

Sauté chicken in oil on medium heat until golden brown, turning once. Place chicken in a baking pan. Lightly cover with aluminum foil and bake for 15 minutes. Remove foil and bake uncovered 5 more minutes to restore crispness to crumb coating.

CHICKEN POT PIE

Down home at its best

BISCUITS

2 cups flour

½ teaspoon salt

4 teaspoons baking powder

½ teaspoon cream of tartar

1 tablespoon sugar

½ cup shortening

⅔ cup milk

FILLING

6 tablespoons butter

6 tablespoons flour

2 cups flavorful chicken broth

1 cup half and half

½ teaspoon pepper

⅛ teaspoon crushed thyme

Salt to taste

4 cups cooked chicken, cut in large chunks

¾ cup pearl onions, cooked

¾ cup frozen peas, thawed

⅓ pound fresh mushrooms (1½ cups), sliced

Serves 6-8.

Preheat oven to 425 degrees.

To prepare biscuits: Mix flour, salt, baking powder, cream of tartar and sugar in a bowl. Cut in shortening until mixture resembles coarse meal. Add milk all at once and stir until dough forms a ball. Knead on a floured board 14 times. Pat to ½-inch thickness and cut with a 2-inch cookie cutter. Bake on a greased baking sheet for 15-20 minutes or until golden brown and done in center. Makes 15 biscuits.

Preheat oven to 375 degrees.

To prepare filling, melt butter in a saucepan and stir in flour. Cook about 2 minutes. Slowly, add the broth, half and half, pepper, thyme and salt to taste. Cook until thick and smooth. Add chicken pieces, pearl onions, peas and mushrooms. Mix gently. Spoon into individual casseroles. Bake 15-20 minutes or until bubbly. Add a biscuit to the top of each casserole and bake another 3 minutes. Reheat extra biscuits 3 minutes before serving.

JUBILEE CHICKEN

A celebration of flavors

8 (4-ounce) chicken breast
   halves, skinned and boned

2 tablespoons melted butter

Salt

Pepper

1 (1-pound) can pitted dark
   cherries with juice

½ cup chili sauce

2 chicken bouillon cubes,
   crumbled

¼ cup dry sherry

½ cup currant jelly

1½ tablespoons cornstarch

2 tablespoons cold water

2 tablespoons brandy or cognac
   (optional)

Cooked hot rice

Serves 8.

Preheat oven to 350 degrees.

Place chicken breast halves in a greased 9
by 13-inch baking pan. Brush tops with
butter and sprinkle with salt and pepper.
Bake at 350 degrees for 20-30 minutes or
until done.

To make sauce, put juice from cherries in a
2-quart saucepan. Set cherries aside. Add
chili sauce, bouillon, sherry and currant
jelly to cherry juice. Heat on medium
until jelly has melted. Mix cornstarch and
water to make a smooth paste. Add to
sauce, stirring, and continue to heat until
clear and slightly thickened. Remove from
heat and add brandy or cognac, if desired,
as well as cherries.

To serve, place baked chicken on a bed of
cooked rice and spoon cherry sauce on
top.

CRISPY HERB-TOPPED CHICKEN

Too easy to be this good

8 (4-ounce) boned and skinned chicken breast halves

8 ounces Swiss cheese, sliced

1 (10-ounce) can cream of chicken soup

¼ cup white wine

2 cups seasoned fine bread crumbs

⅓ cup melted butter

8 teaspoons almond slivers

SEASONED BREAD CRUMBS

2 cups fine dry bread crumbs

½ teaspoon sage

¼ teaspoon savory

½ teaspoon onion powder

1 tablespoon dried parsley flakes

Serves 8.

Preheat oven to 350 degrees.

Place chicken in greased 9 x 13-inch baking pan. Cover with slices of cheese. Mix soup and wine. Spread evenly over chicken. Combine ingredients for seasoned bread crumbs. Distribute crumbs over the top. Drizzle with melted butter. Sprinkle with almonds. Bake 30-35 minutes or until done.

TURKEY SCALLOPINI

½ cup olive oil, divided

2 cups thinly sliced onions

¼ pound mushrooms, sliced

1½ pounds raw turkey breast

⅓ cup flour

1 teaspoon salt

¼ teaspoon pepper

1 cup chicken broth

1 large clove garlic, minced

3 tablespoons lemon juice

¼ cup Parmesan cheese

Fresh chopped parsley

2 - 3 cups cooked rice

Serves 6.

Preheat oven to 350 degrees.

Sauté onions and mushrooms in ¼ cup oil. Remove from pan and drain.

Cut turkey breast in strips ¼ inch thick, 1 inch wide and 2 inches long. Combine flour, salt and pepper in a plastic bag. Add turkey strips and shake to coat. Remove, shaking off excess flour. Brown turkey strips in remaining oil. Place turkey, onions and mushrooms in a 2-quart casserole.

Add chicken broth, garlic and lemon juice to browning pan, stirring to scrape up meat juices. Pour over turkey and vegetables. Sprinkle with Parmesan cheese. Bake covered at 350 degrees for 20-30 minutes. Serve over rice and sprinkle with parsley.

VEAL BOLOGNESE

An elegant, rich alternative to traditional lasagne. Can be made ahead.

VEAL SAUCE

2 tablespoons olive oil

2 tablespoons margarine or butter

½ cup chopped onion

½ cup chopped celery

½ cup grated carrot

1 pound ground veal

1 cup dry white wine

1 (15-ounce) can Roma tomatoes (and liquid), pureed or blended

2 tablespoons tomato paste

½ cup half and half

CREAM SAUCE

½ cup butter or margarine

½ cup flour

2 cups chicken broth

2 cups milk

⅛ teaspoon nutmeg

12 lasagne noodles (about ½ pound)

¼ pound mozzarella cheese, grated

1 cup Parmesan cheese

Serves 9-10.

To prepare veal sauce, heat olive oil and margarine or butter in a large frying pan. Add onions, celery and carrots and cook until onion is limp. Crumble ground veal into pan, stirring until meat loses its pink color. Add white wine and boil, stirring over medium heat until wine evaporates. Reduce heat and add tomatoes, tomato paste and half and half. Simmer, uncovered, stirring often until sauce reduces to 4 cups (about 15 minutes). Cool. Use or cover and refrigerate up to 2 days, or freeze.

To prepare cream sauce, melt butter or margarine in a saucepan over medium heat. Add flour and cook, stirring for 2 minutes. Gradually add chicken broth and milk, stirring constantly until sauce has thickened. Add nutmeg. Cool.

Preheat oven to 350 degrees.

Cook lasagne noodles per package directions. Rinse. Grease a 9 by 13-inch baking dish. Arrange 3 noodles lengthwise on bottom of dish. Spread 1 cup of cream sauce evenly over noodles, covering thinly. Carefully spread 1⅓ cups veal sauce over the cream sauce. Sprinkle ¼ cup Parmesan cheese and ⅓ cup mozzarella cheese over sauce. Repeat these layers twice. For the fourth (top) layer, start with the lasagne noodles. Use only the remaining cream sauce and ¼ cup Parmesan cheese. If made ahead, cover and chill up to 1 day.

Bake uncovered for about 50-60 minutes (more if very cold) until heated through. Let stand 20 minutes before cutting.

BEEF BOURGUIGNON

¼ pound salt pork, thinly sliced

¼ cup brandy

⅛ teaspoon pepper

½ cup flour

1½ teaspoons salt

½ teaspoon pepper

Dash cayenne pepper

3 pounds stew meat, cut into
   1½-inch cubes

Butter for sautéeing

4 medium onions, chopped

2 cups beef broth

1½ cups Burgundy wine

½ teaspoon thyme

½ teaspoon marjoram

1 pound fresh mushrooms, sliced

Parsley

Serves 8-10.

Preheat oven to 350 degrees.

Marinate salt pork in brandy with ⅛ teaspoon pepper for 30-60 minutes.

Combine flour, salt, pepper and cayenne. Dredge beef in this mixture. Melt some butter in a heavy skillet and brown stew meat on all sides. Transfer browned beef to a deep baking pan. Sauté chopped onions in butter and add to the meat. Add salt pork and brandy. Deglaze sauté pan with ¼ cup beef broth and add to beef. Add wine, thyme, marjoram and the remaining beef broth. Cover tightly and bake for 2-2½ hours or until meat is tender. Add more wine or broth if liquid evaporates.

Remove salt pork, add mushrooms and then bake uncovered for an additional ½ hour, stirring once or twice.

Serve over noodles, rice or with oven-baked red potatoes. Garnish with parsley.

BEEF MONTE CARLO

Don't skip the anchovies

2½ pounds lean beef

2 tablespoons margarine

1 cup chopped onion

2 cloves garlic, minced

2 cups red wine

1 tablespoon grated orange
   peel

½ teaspoon thyme

2 bay leaves

1 beef bouillon cube, crumbled

2 tablespoons tomato paste

4 anchovies, chopped

¼ cup milk

3 carrots, cut in ½-inch chunks

Curly noodles, cooked

Chives or parsley, chopped
   (optional)

Serves 8.

Preheat oven to 350 degrees.

Cut beef in strips, as for stir fry, and sauté in margarine until browned, using a large oven-proof kettle. Add onion, garlic, wine, orange peel, seasonings, bouillon and tomato paste.

Soak anchovies in milk for 10 minutes. Drain and discard milk. Add anchovies to beef mixture.

Add carrots and stir to mix ingredients. Cover and bake for 1½ hours. Serve on curly noodles and garnish with chopped chives or parsley.

BEEF PROVENCALE

Just add French bread and a green salad

6 slices bacon

1 pound lean beef (chuck), cut in 1-inch cubes

½ cup flour

1 teaspoon salt

1 (10-ounce) can beef consommé

1 cup dry red wine

1 small clove garlic, minced

½ teaspoon thyme

2 tablespoons chopped fresh parsley

6 medium new potatoes, cut in chunks

5 carrots, sliced lengthwise in 2-inch strips

12 small white onions, peeled

⅓ pound fresh mushrooms, sliced

Parsley

Serves 4-6.

Preheat oven to 350 degrees.

Fry bacon in a saucepan on medium heat until crisp. Remove bacon to use later. Dredge beef cubes in a mixture of flour and salt. Sauté beef in bacon grease until it has browned. Transfer beef to a 4-quart baking dish. Put consommé, wine, garlic, thyme and parsley into a blender and blend until solid ingredients are pureed. Pour over beef. Cover and bake in oven for 1 hour or until beef is almost tender. Add potatoes, carrots, onions and mushrooms. Bake 1 more hour until done. Uncover the last 15 minutes, if you wish less liquid. Crumble bacon and scatter on top. Sprinkle with additional chopped fresh parsley.

BEEF IN PHYLLO

A taco in a party wrap

1 pound ground beef

½ pound bulk pork sausage

1 medium onion, chopped

1 large clove garlic, minced

¼ teaspoon salt

¼ teaspoon pepper

½ teaspoon chili powder

3 cups grated Monterey Jack cheese

1 (4-ounce) can diced green chiles, drained

1 (4-ounce) can sliced ripe olives

¾ pound phyllo dough

½ cup butter, melted

Paprika

1 cup sour cream (optional)

1 medium ripe avocado, peeled and sliced (optional)

Salsa (optional)

Guacamole (optional)

Serves 8.

Preheat oven to 350 degrees.

Brown beef and sausage then add onion, garlic, salt, pepper and chili powder. Cook about 12 minutes and drain off fat. Cool. Mix cheese, chiles and olives with the cooled meat. To keep phyllo from drying out while using, unroll package and place on a large tray. Cover with plastic wrap and then a damp towel. Cover each time you remove sheets of phyllo.

To make beef phyllo packets, place 2 sheets of phyllo together on a tray and brush top sheet with melted butter. Place ⅛ of the meat mixture 2 inches from 1 end, in the center. Fold the 2 inches of phyllo over, then fold both sides evenly toward the center. Roll to form a package. Repeat until 8 packages are formed.

Place in buttered baking dish and brush top and sides of package with melted butter.

Bake 15-20 minutes until flaky and golden. Sprinkle with paprika. Serve with sour cream, avocado slices or guacamole and salsa.

Moussaka

1½ pounds eggplant

2 tablespoons olive oil

Meat Sauce

2 tablespoons butter

1 cup finely chopped onion

1 teaspoon minced garlic

1½ pounds ground lamb or beef

⅛ teaspoon ground cinnamon

½ teaspoon salt

¼ teaspoon pepper

½ cup crushed tomatoes

¼ cup tomato paste

¼ cup dry red wine

¼ cup chopped parsley

Cheese Sauce

3 tablespoons butter

3 tablespoons flour

¼ teaspoon salt

2 cups milk

2 eggs, slightly beaten

⅛ teaspoon ground nutmeg

½ cup ricotta cheese

½ cup sour cream

¼ cup grated Parmesan

Serves 8.

Preheat oven to 350 degrees.

Peel eggplant and slice into ½-inch slices. Brown both sides of eggplant in oil. Set aside.

To prepare meat sauce, heat butter in skillet, sauté onion and add garlic and meat. Cook until meat has browned. Add cinnamon, salt and pepper. Stir well. Add tomatoes, tomato paste, wine and parsley. Cook until moisture has evaporated.

To prepare cheese sauce, heat butter in saucepan and add flour and salt. Stir with wire whisk. When smooth add milk and continue cooking and stirring until slightly thickened. Add eggs, nutmeg, ricotta and sour cream. Blend well.

Butter a 9 by 13-inch baking dish. Place eggplant in dish. Spoon meat sauce over and smooth top. Sprinkle with half of the Parmesan cheese. Add cheese sauce and smooth top. Sprinkle with remaining Parmesan and bake for 40-45 minutes or until custard layer has set. Let rest for 10 minutes, then cut in squares and serve.

REUBEN CASSEROLE

A Saint Patrick's Day special

2½ cups sauerkraut

½ pound cooked corned beef, cut in ¼-inch chunks

4 teaspoons Dijon mustard

1½ tablespoons butter or margarine

1½ tablespoons flour

1 cup chicken broth

2 cups grated Swiss cheese

1 cup rye bread crumbs

2 tablespoons melted butter or margarine

Paprika

Serves 4.

Preheat oven to 350 degrees.

Drain the sauerkraut and set aside. Combine corned beef chunks and Dijon mustard.

Melt margarine over medium heat in a small saucepan. Stir in flour. Cook for 1-2 minutes. Gradually add chicken broth. Continue cooking and stirring until broth has thickened. Remove from heat.

Butter a small oven-proof casserole. Place half of the sauerkraut in the bottom, adding all the corned beef chunks on top. Sprinkle with half of the Swiss cheese, then cover with the rest of the sauerkraut. Pour all of the thickened broth on top. Sprinkle with the remaining cheese and the rye bread crumbs that have been mixed with the melted butter or margarine. Bake uncovered for 20-30 minutes, or until heated through and browned on top. Sprinkle with paprika.

SAVORY BEEF RAGOUT

Serve with a green salad and hearty bread

1 pound lean beef cubes (cross-rib or chuck eye), cut in small cubes

¼ cup chopped onions

2 tablespoons margarine

2 tablespoons flour

1 (10-ounce) can beef consommé

2 cups water

1 tablespoon tomato paste

1 beef bouillon cube

1 teaspoon thyme

1 bay leaf

¼ teaspoon garlic powder

⅛ teaspoon Tabasco

⅛ teaspoon pepper

½ cup Burgundy wine

2 medium carrots, cut in small chunks

3 - 4 small red potatoes, unpeeled, cut in ¾-inch chunks

Chopped Parsley

Serves 6.

Melt margarine in a large heavy pot. Dredge the beef with flour and brown on medium heat. Add onions and sauté lightly. Add beef consommé, water, tomato paste, bouillon cube, seasonings and Burgundy wine. Simmer, covered, on low heat for 1 hour or until beef is tender. Remove bay leaf.

Add carrots and potatoes. Bring to a boil, then lower heat and simmer for 20-30 minutes until vegetables are tender. Serve in deep soup bowls and sprinkle with chopped parsley.

SUMMER LASAGNE

Zucchini replaces the pasta in this light summer dish

3/4 pound lean ground beef

1/2 cup finely chopped onion

2 cloves garlic, crushed

1/2 cup diced green pepper

1/4 cup grated carrot

1 (16-ounce) can tomato sauce

1/2 teaspoon oregano

1/2 teaspoon basil

Salt and pepper to taste

5 medium zucchini, unpeeled

1 egg, beaten

8 ounces ricotta cheese

1 1/2 cups grated mozzarella cheese

1/8 cup grated Parmesan cheese

Serves 8.

Preheat oven to 350 degrees.

Butter an 8 by 12-inch baking dish.

Brown beef, breaking it up. Drain off fat. Add onion, garlic, green pepper, carrot, tomato sauce and seasonings and simmer 10 minutes.

Slice zucchini about 1/4 inch thick, and arrange half of the slices in baking dish. Combine egg and ricotta cheese. Spread all of the ricotta cheese mixture over zucchini. Spoon half of the meat sauce over the top. Sprinkle with half of the mozzarella. Layer with remaining zucchini and mozzarella. Add the rest of the meat sauce. Sprinkle top with Parmesan cheese.

Bake for 40 minutes. Let stand 10 minutes before cutting and serving.

Parmesan Meatballs with Pasta

No-fry meatballs; oven browned

Meatballs

1 pound ground beef

½ cup soft bread crumbs

½ cup milk

1 egg, slightly beaten

¾ cup grated Parmesan cheese

¾ cup minced onion

1 teaspoon salt

½ teaspoon pepper

Sauce

3 tablespoons butter

¼ cup flour

1 cup beef consommé

½ cup sour cream

½ cup dry white wine

Pasta

1 pound pasta, cooked as directed

Butter

Chopped parsley

Serves 6.

Preheat oven to 350 degrees.

Mix all meatball ingredients thoroughly and form into balls the size of walnuts or golf balls, depending on size wanted. Brown in oven on rack 15-20 minutes. Do not let meatballs cook dry.

To prepare sauce, melt butter and add flour, cooking together for 2 minutes. Add beef consommé and heat until thickened, stirring constantly. Add sour cream and white wine and heat 5 minutes more.

To prepare pasta, toss with butter and parsley. Arrange meatballs on top of pasta and pour sauce over all.

SWEET AND SOUR MEATBALLS

1½ pounds lean ground beef

¾ cup rolled oats

1 cup evaporated milk

3 tablespoons chopped onion

1½ teaspoons salt

¼ teaspoon pepper

¼ cup margarine or oil

SAUCE

2 tablespoons Worcestershire sauce

3 tablespoons cider vinegar

1 cup catsup

½ cup water

2 tablespoons sugar

⅓ cup chopped onion

3 cups cooked rice

Serves 8.

Mix beef, oats, milk, the 3 tablespoons onion, salt and pepper. Let stand 10 minutes. Roll the meat into 1½-inch balls. Brown in oil.

To prepare sauce combine Worcestershire sauce, vinegar, catsup, water, sugar and ⅓ cup onion. Add to meatballs and cook slowly for about 30 minutes, stirring occasionally. Serve over rice.

FLORENTINE HAM CREPES

Very impressive for a lunch/brunch

8 crepes (8 inches in diameter)*

6 thin slices deli ham

⅔ cup whipping cream (not whipped)

½ cup grated Gruyere cheese

½ cup toasted coarsely chopped pistachio nuts

SPINACH FILLING

1 bunch spinach, cleaned, stems removed

2 tablespoons butter

2 tablespoons flour

1 cup milk

¼ teaspoon salt

⅛ teaspoon pepper

⅛ teaspoon nutmeg

MUSHROOM FILLING

1 tablespoon butter

1 tablespoon oil

2 tablespoons minced shallots

½ pound mushrooms, thinly sliced

Salt and pepper

Serves 4.

Preheat oven to 350 degrees.

Prepare spinach and mushroom filling first.

To assemble, use a round 10-inch oven-proof dish. Lightly butter bottom and lay in 1 crepe. Cover with 2 thin slices of ham. Drizzle 1 tablespoon of cream over ham. Layer with another crepe. Spread with half of the Spinach Filling and drizzle with 1 tablespoon cream. Cover with another crepe, spread half of the Mushroom Filling over it and drizzle with 1 tablespoon cream. Repeat this process for crepes 4, 5 and 6. For layer 7, do a ham layer then add the last crepe. Spoon remaining cream on top. Place in oven and bake 15 minutes. Remove from oven. Add grated Gruyere and chopped pistachios. Place under broiler 2-3 minutes until cheese is melted. Cut into 4 wedges.

To make Spinach Filling, blanch spinach in lightly salted water for 1 minute. Remove and drain very well. Chop spinach in processor. In a saucepan, melt butter over low heat and stir in flour to make a roux. Slowly add milk and whisk until mixture thickens. Add seasonings and stir in spinach. Set aside.

To make Mushroom Filling, heat butter and oil in sauté pan. Add shallots and sauté 1-2 minutes. Add mushrooms and cook 10 minutes or until mushroom juices have evaporated. Lightly season with salt and pepper. Set aside.

*See BASIC CREPE RECIPE page 131.

ASPARAGUS CORDON BLEU CREPES

A springtime favorite

16 large or 32 small asparagus
    spears

16 crepes*

16 (¾-ounce) ham slices

3 - 4 cups grated Swiss cheese

Paprika

Dijon mustard (optional)

SAUCE

¼ cup butter

¼ cup flour

1 cup half and half

1 cup chicken broth

¼ teaspoon white pepper

¼ teaspoon salt

⅛ teaspoon cayenne pepper

¾ cup grated Parmesan cheese

Serves 8.

Preheat oven to 350 degrees.

Cook asparagus until barely tender. Drain and cool under running water.

Place 1 slice of ham on each crepe. Spread ham lightly with Dijon mustard if desired. Top with 3-4 tablespoons of cheese. Place 1 large or 2 small asparagus spears on top of ham and cheese. Roll. Place 2 rolls per serving, seam side down, in individual casseroles or use 9 by 13-inch baking pan for entire recipe. Make sauce and pour over crepes. Bake 20-30 minutes or until hot and bubbly. Sprinkle with paprika.

To prepare sauce, melt butter. Add flour and cook for 3 minutes, stirring. Add half and half and broth. Cook over medium heat, stirring constantly, until sauce begins to thicken. Add seasonings and cheese and continue to cook 5 more minutes.

*See BASIC CREPE RECIPE page 131.

HAM CANNELLONI

Ham and spinach with an Italian accent

FILLING

8 ounces cubed ham (1½ cups)

1 (10-ounce) package frozen chopped spinach, thawed

1 pound ricotta cheese

2 egg yolks, beaten

¾ cup grated Parmesan cheese

½ teaspoon crushed fennel seed

¾ teaspoon oregano

10 egg roll wrappers

1¼ cups grated Monterey Jack cheese

SAUCE

4½ cups canned tomatoes, undrained

2 tablespoons salad oil

1¼ cups finely chopped onion

2 cloves garlic, minced

1 tablespoon dried mint

1½ teaspoons dried basil

2 cups chicken broth

¼ teaspoon salt

Serves 10.

Preheat oven to 350 degrees.

To prepare sauce, pulse tomatoes in food processor 5-6 times. Set aside. Sauté onion and garlic in oil until limp. Add tomatoes, seasonings and chicken broth. Simmer, uncovered, stirring occasionally. Cook about 15 minutes.

Mince ham in food processor. Squeeze spinach well. Combine and mix ham, spinach, ricotta cheese, egg yolks, Parmesan cheese and seasonings.

Spread ⅓ of the sauce in a buttered 9 by 13-inch shallow baking dish. Cut egg roll wrappers in half. Mound ¼ cup filling along short end of each egg roll wrapper and roll. Place rolls seam side down, slightly apart, on top of sauce. Cover with remaining sauce, spreading evenly. Sprinkle with Monterey Jack cheese. Bake for 30-40 minutes or until hot and bubbly. Allow to stand a few minutes before serving.

CRUSTLESS HAM AND ARTICHOKE QUICHE

One of Albertina's exceptional recipes

⅓ pound mushrooms, sliced

2 tablespoons butter or margarine

4 eggs, well beaten

1 cup sour cream or yogurt

1 cup small curd cottage cheese, blended in processor

½ cup grated Parmesan cheese

¼ cup flour

1 teaspoon onion powder

⅛ teaspoon salt

4 drops Tabasco

1½ cups cubed, cooked ham

2 cups grated Monterey Jack cheese

¾ cup artichoke hearts, quartered

Serves 8.

Preheat oven to 350 degrees.

Sauté mushrooms in butter. Drain on paper towel.

Blend eggs, sour cream, cottage cheese, Parmesan cheese, flour and seasonings in a large bowl. Add mushrooms, ham, Monterey Jack cheese and artichokes, mixing well. Pour into greased 10-inch quiche pan or pie plate. Bake 35-45 minutes or until knife inserted in center comes out clean. Allow to stand 5 minutes before cutting.

Variations include Shrimp Quiche and Quiche Lorraine.

To prepare Shrimp Quiche, omit ham and artichokes. Increase mushrooms to ½ pound and salt to ¼ teaspoon. Add ½ pound small cooked shrimp.

To prepare Quiche Lorraine, omit ham and artichokes. Increase mushrooms to ½ pound. Add 12 ounces of bacon which has been crisply fried, drained on paper towels and crumbled in small pieces. If desired, add ¼ cup sliced green onions and sauté with mushrooms.

HAM AND ARTICHOKE PIE IN A RICE CRUST

This has some crust!

⅓ cup uncooked rice

¾ cup water

1 teaspoon chicken bouillon

1 teaspoon Italian seasoning

1 cup cubed cooked ham

¾ cup quartered unmarinated artichoke hearts

1 cup grated Swiss cheese

2 tablespoons chopped green onion

2 tablespoons chopped green pepper

4 large eggs, beaten

1 cup milk

¼ teaspoon salt

⅛ teaspoon white pepper

¼ teaspoon Worcestershire sauce

4 drops Tabasco

Serves 6.

Cook rice in water to which chicken bouillon and Italian seasoning have been added. Cover and cook until all liquid is absorbed. Cool to lukewarm temperature.

Preheat oven to 350 degrees.

Press rice onto the bottom and sides of a greased 9-inch pie pan. Sprinkle with ham, artichokes, cheese, onion and green pepper.

Combine eggs, milk, salt, pepper, Worcestershire sauce and Tabasco. Pour over ingredients in pie pan. Bake 30-40 minutes or until knife inserted in center comes out clean.

May be prepared in advance and refrigerated up to a few hours before baking.

Zucchini Torta

Filling

4 slices bacon, cooked and crumbled

2 tablespoons bacon drippings

1 pound zucchini, thinly sliced

1 cup chopped onion

2 cloves garlic, minced

7 large eggs

1 cup sour cream

1¼ teaspoons salt

2 cups cooked cold rice

12 ounces sharp cheddar cheese, grated

Pastry

1 cup flour

6 tablespoons butter

1½ tablespoons vegetable shortening

¼ teaspoon salt

1½ tablespoons ice water

Serves 8.

Preheat oven to 375 degrees.

To prepare pastry, combine all ingredients except water. Blend well with pastry cutter. Add water. Form dough ball, knead lightly. Form again into ball and chill. Press into a 10-inch springform pan, covering bottom and 2 inches up the sides.

Heat bacon drippings. Add zucchini, onion and garlic and sauté over medium heat for 15 minutes. Drain well.

Beat eggs, add sour cream and salt and beat again. Stir in rice, cheese, vegetables and bacon. Turn into unbaked pastry shell and smooth the top. Bake about 55 minutes or until golden and set. Allow to rest 5 minutes, then loosen rim of pan. (Can be baked without crust in a 1½-quart casserole.)

FLORENTINE HAM ROULADE

1 (10-ounce) package frozen chopped spinach, thawed and squeezed dry

1 cup cornbread stuffing mix, prepared according to directions

1 cup sour cream

⅓ cup Parmesan cheese

12 thin slices of ham

Paprika

Parmesan cheese (topping)

SAUCE

¼ cup butter

¼ cup flour

2 cups milk

¼ cup grated sharp cheddar cheese

Serves 6.

Preheat oven to 350 degrees.

Combine spinach, stuffing, sour cream and ⅓ cup Parmesan cheese. Place ¼ cup of this mixture on each slice of ham. Roll up and place seam side down on a greased baking pan. Make sauce and pour over ham rolls. Sprinkle with paprika and Parmesan cheese. Bake 25-30 minutes or until hot and bubbly.

To prepare sauce, melt butter, add flour and gradually stir in milk. Continue to stir and cook until thickened. Remove from heat and stir in cheese.

BAKED BARBEQUED PORK LOIN

This sauce will especially delight the chutney lover

½ cup chutney

¼ cup lemon juice

2 teaspoons brown sugar

2 teaspoons Worcestershire sauce

½ cup water

½ cup catsup

1 pound pork loin, sliced in 15 pieces

Serves 5.

Preheat oven to 350 degrees.

Pulse chutney in blender until smooth. Place all ingredients in a saucepan except pork and bring to a boil. Lower heat and simmer for 20 minutes, stirring occasionally.

Place pork in baking dish and cover with sauce. Bake uncovered for 20-30 minutes. May be served over parsley rice.

STUFFED HAM ROLLS

Extraordinary combination

1¼ cups cooked rice

2 tablespoons minced parsley

¾ cup toasted slivered almonds

⅛ teaspoon pepper

¼ teaspoon poultry seasoning

12 slices (medium to thin) boiled
   ham

Parmesan cheese

Paprika

CHICKEN SAUCE

4 tablespoons butter

4 tablespoons flour

2 cups milk

⅛ teaspoon salt

⅛ teaspoon white pepper

1½ cups cooked and diced
   chicken breasts

Serves 6.

Preheat oven to 350 degrees.

Prepare Chicken Sauce. Melt butter and add flour. Blend well. Cook 2-3 minutes, stirring constantly. Gradually whisk in milk. Add seasonings. Cook and stir until thickened. Add chicken and remove from heat. Chicken Sauce will be used in rice filling as well as over the top of the ham rolls.

Combine rice, parsley, almonds, pepper, poultry seasoning and ¼ cup of the Chicken Sauce. Lay ham slices flat and fill each with a scant ¼ cup rice mixture. Roll. Place 2 rolls in individual ramekins, seam side down. Cover each serving with ½ cup Chicken Sauce and top each with 1 tablespoon Parmesan cheese. Bake 20 minutes or until hot and bubbly. Sprinkle with paprika before serving.

SAVORY PORK TENDERLOIN

A good marriage of flavors

2 (1-pound) pork tenderloins

¼ teaspoon salt

¼ teaspoon pepper

¼ teaspoon marjoram

1 cup chopped onion

2 bay leaves

1 cup chicken broth

¼ cup dry white wine

4 cups cooked orzo

Paprika

SAUCE

⅓ cup margarine

⅓ cup flour

1 cup chicken broth

1 chicken bouillon cube

1 beef bouillon cube

1 cup dry white wine

2 cups sour cream

1 cup sauerkraut, undrained,
    blended in processor

½ teaspoon marjoram

1 tablespoon minced chives

¼ teaspoon black pepper

½ pound mushrooms, sliced

Serves 10.

Preheat oven to 350 degrees.

Slice pork in ½-inch slices. Place slices in 9 by 12-inch baking pan. Sprinkle meat with salt, pepper and marjoram. Scatter onion on top and add bay leaves. Pour chicken broth and wine over all. Cover tightly and bake 30-35 minutes or until pork is thoroughly cooked.

While meat bakes, prepare sauce. Melt margarine in a 2-quart saucepan and stir in flour. Cook 2-3 minutes. Slowly add chicken broth to which extra bouillon cubes have been added. Add wine. Cook on medium heat, stirring constantly, until sauce thickens. Add sour cream, sauerkraut and seasonings. Cook and stir until sauce is hot and thickened. Add mushrooms.

When pork is done, uncover, remove bay leaves and drain off liquid.

In each of 10 individual greased casseroles, measure a rounded ⅓ cup of orzo. Spoon ¼ cup sauce onto orzo. Place 3-5 slices of meat on top, some onion included. Add ⅓ cup sauce over pork, covering completely. Sprinkle with paprika. Bake 20-25 minutes or until hot and bubbly.

MEDALLIONS OF PORK SUPREME

2 (1-pound) pork tenderloins

2 cloves garlic, slightly crushed

2 teaspoons paprika

4 tablespoons butter

4 cups cooked orzo or rice

3 - 4 tomatoes, cut in wedges

8 slices bacon, crisply cooked,
    drained and crumbled

Paprika

SAUCE

¼ cup pan drippings

¼ cup flour

1 cup half and half

1 cup beef broth

½ teaspoon salt

¼ teaspoon pepper

8 ounces mushrooms, sliced and
    slightly sautéed

Serves 10.

Preheat oven to 350 degrees.

Rub meat with garlic and sprinkle with paprika. Brown meat in butter. Turn heat to low. Cover and cook 15-20 minutes. Remove meat from pan and slice in ½-inch pieces. Save pan with drippings.

Place ⅓ cup of rice or orzo in each of 10 individual greased casseroles. Alternate 3 slices of meat with 3 tomato wedges on top of rice or orzo. Top each serving with ⅓ cup sauce and sprinkle with crumbled bacon and extra paprika. Bake uncovered for 20-25 minutes.

To prepare sauce, add flour to pan drippings and cook for 1-2 minutes. Add half and half and beef broth, stirring until thickened. Add salt and pepper. Stir in sautéed mushrooms.

SALMON QUICHE WITH ALMOND-CRUMB CRUST

Spectacular

CRUST

1 cup whole-wheat flour

1 cup grated sharp cheddar
   cheese

½ cup chopped almonds

½ teaspoon salt

¼ teaspoon paprika

⅓ cup oil

FILLING

1 (15¼ -ounce) can salmon

1 cup grated sharp cheddar
   cheese

½ cup finely chopped onion

3 eggs, beaten

1 cup sour cream

½ cup mayonnaise

1 tablespoon dill weed

5 drops Tabasco

Serves 8.

Preheat oven to 400 degrees.

To prepare crust, combine all ingredients
except oil. Mix well. Slowly pour oil over
top and continue mixing. Press crumb
crust into bottom and sides of a 10-inch
pie tin. Bake 10 minutes. Remove from
oven and reduce heat to 325 degrees.

To prepare filling, remove bones and skin
from salmon. Break salmon meat into
small flakes. Add grated cheese and
chopped onion. Mix well. Combine
beaten eggs with sour cream, mayonnaise,
dill and Tabasco. Mix well and add to
salmon mixture.

Pour into baked crust and bake 45-60
minutes or until set. Let cool for 10
minutes before cutting.

CRUSTLESS BROCCOLI QUICHE WITH SHRIMP SAUCE

Tasty with or without the sauce

QUICHE

½ pound fresh mushrooms, sliced

2 tablespoons butter

4 eggs, beaten lightly

1 cup cottage cheese, blended in food processor

1 cup sour cream

½ cup grated Parmesan cheese

¼ cup flour

1 teaspoon onion powder

¼ teaspoon salt

4 drops Tabasco

2 cups grated Monterey Jack cheese

1½ cups broccoli, fresh and lightly steamed, or thawed, drained frozen broccoli

SHRIMP SAUCE

3 tablespoons margarine

3 tablespoons flour

½ cup chicken broth

½ cup milk

½ cup sour cream

1 teaspoon lemon juice

¼ teaspoon curry powder (optional)

1 cup small cooked shrimp

Serves 8.

Preheat oven to 350 degrees.

Sauté mushrooms in butter. Drain well. Combine beaten eggs, blended cottage cheese, sour cream, Parmesan cheese, flour, onion powder, salt and Tabasco. Mix well. Add cheese. Cut broccoli into bite-sized pieces and add to egg mixture. Pour quiche mixture into greased 10-inch quiche or pie pan. Bake 35-45 minutes or until center is set. Cool 5 minutes. Cut and serve with Shrimp Sauce.

To prepare sauce, melt margarine in a saucepan. Add flour, cook, and stir for 2 minutes over low heat. Add chicken broth and milk. Heat, stirring constantly, until sauce thickens. Add sour cream, lemon juice and curry powder. Stir and remove from heat. Just before serving, add shrimp and reheat carefully. Serve over individual portions of quiche. You may add more curry powder if desired.

BAKED SOLE WITH ARTICHOKE HEARTS

Heart and sole

8 Dover sole fillets (2 ounces each or 1 pound total)

1½ cups cooked rice

FILLING

1 teaspoon margarine

½ cup finely minced onion

1 clove garlic, minced

2 tablespoons dry white wine

¼ teaspoon thyme

¼ teaspoon Italian seasoning

1 teaspoon dried parsley

1 (4-ounce) can artichoke hearts, drained and diced

TOPPING

3 tablespoons lemon juice

½ cup light mayonnaise

2 tablespoons grated Parmesan cheese

Paprika

Serves 4.

Preheat oven to 350 degrees.

Prepare filling. Sauté onions and garlic in margarine until soft. Add wine, thyme, Italian seasoning, parsley and diced artichokes. Heat for 2-3 minutes until wine has evaporated.

Place a layer of rice in greased individual ramekins or in a shallow baking dish. Lay raw fish over rice, using half of the fillets. Spread artichoke filling on top of fillets. Lay the rest of the fillets over artichoke mixture.

Combine lemon juice and mayonnaise. Spread over top of fish. Sprinkle with Parmesan cheese.

Bake 20-25 minutes. Sprinkle with paprika.

FILLET OF FISH SUPREME

Simple and good

2 tablespoons butter

2 tablespoons lemon juice

1 cup sour cream

1½ pounds firm white fish

Salt

Pepper

½ medium onion, thinly sliced
and divided into rings

1½ cups grated medium
cheddar cheese

Serves 6.

Preheat oven to 350 degrees.

Melt butter. Add lemon juice and sour cream. Sprinkle uncooked fish with salt and pepper and place in greased casserole. Top with onion rings. Pour sour cream mixture over fish and sprinkle with cheese. Bake 35 minutes or until fish flakes with a fork.

FISHERMAN'S FAVORITE

A weight-watcher's delight

1 pound lingcod or red snapper,
deboned

Salt

Pepper

9 cooked asparagus spears

¼ cup chicken broth

¼ cup tomato juice

1 teaspoon horseradish

¼ teaspoon garlic salt

2 teaspoons grated onion

1 teaspoon sugar

2 teaspoons cornstarch

1 tablespoon cold water

½ cup Monterey Jack cheese

Serves 3.

Preheat oven to 325 degrees.

Cut fish into 3 portions and place in buttered, shallow baking dish. Sprinkle with salt and pepper. Lay 3 asparagus spears on top of each fillet.

In a small saucepan, combine chicken broth, tomato juice, horseradish, garlic salt, onion and sugar. Simmer over medium heat for 3-4 minutes. Combine cornstarch and cold water. Stir into tomato mixture. Cook 1-2 minutes more or until sauce thickens. Pour sauce over asparagus and fish. Sprinkle with cheese.

Bake 30 minutes.

HERB-TOPPED FISH

Popular at Albertina's

8 fillets of salmon, halibut,
    lingcod or snapper, deboned,
    1 - 1½ inches thick

¾ cup mayonnaise

½ cup sour cream

½ cup grated Parmesan cheese

4 tablespoons chopped chives

2 tablespoons chopped parsley

½ teaspoon onion salt

½ teaspoon dried dill

½ teaspoon dry mustard

⅛ teaspoon black pepper

Paprika

Serves 8.

Preheat oven to 350 degrees.

Place uncooked fish fillets in a buttered, shallow baking dish.

Blend by hand all remaining ingredients except paprika. Spread ¼ cup mixture on top of each fillet.

Bake 20 minutes or until fish flakes. Sprinkle with paprika before serving.

SAVORY CHEESE-TOPPED FISH

2 pounds thick white fish fillets

2 cups white wine

2 cups water

3 tablespoons butter

¼ pound mushrooms, sliced

2 tablespoons minced green onions

¾ teaspoon salt

½ teaspoon basil

¼ teaspoon lemon pepper

1 medium tomato, chopped

1 cup grated cheddar cheese

1 egg, beaten

Serves 8.

Preheat oven to 350 degrees.

Poach fish in wine and water until fish barely flakes. Drain well.

Melt butter and sauté mushrooms and onions. Remove from heat and cool. Combine salt, basil, lemon pepper, tomato, cheese and egg. Add mushrooms and onions. Mix well.

Place fish fillets in a buttered, shallow baking dish. Top each fillet with some of the mushroom and cheese mixture. Bake 15 minutes or until cheese is melted.

SOLE FLORENTINE WITH MORNAY SAUCE

½ cup sliced celery

⅓ cup chopped onion

¼ cup water

¼ teaspoon salt

⅛ teaspoon pepper

1 cup sliced mushrooms

1 cup frozen chopped broccoli, thawed

½ cup frozen chopped spinach, thawed and well drained

½ cup herb stuffing mix

6 (4-ounce) sole fillets

2 tablespoons margarine, melted

2½ cups cooked rice

Parmesan cheese

Paprika

MORNAY SAUCE

2 tablespoons margarine

2 tablespoons flour

1 teaspoon chicken bouillon granules

⅛ teaspoon nutmeg

1 cup milk

2 tablespoons dry white wine

Serves 6.

Preheat oven to 350 degrees.

To make stuffing, combine celery, onion, water, salt and pepper in a medium saucepan. Cover and cook over low heat until vegetables are slightly tender. Add mushrooms and cook 5 more minutes. Add broccoli and spinach. Stir in herb stuffing mix.

Lay out sole fillets on a tray. Divide stuffing among fillets, placing it in the center of each fillet. Lay ends loosely over stuffing. Place seam side down in a greased baking dish. Brush tops with melted margarine.

Bake 20-25 minutes or until fish flakes and stuffing is hot in the center. Serve with rice and top with Mornay Sauce. Sprinkle Parmesan cheese and paprika on top.

To prepare Mornay Sauce, melt margarine in a 1-quart saucepan. Stir in flour, bouillon granules and nutmeg. Cook over medium heat for 2 minutes. Add milk and heat, stirring constantly, until thick. Add white wine. Spoon over stuffed sole fillets.

BAKED BAY SCALLOPS

For an easy company dinner, serve with GREENS JULIUS

2 tablespoons butter or margarine

2 tablespoons diced onion

1 pound fresh bay scallops

⅓ pound fresh mushrooms, sliced

2½ cups cooked warm rice

3 cups broccoli florets, lightly steamed and refreshed in cold water

Garlic Butter slices

GARLIC BUTTER

1 cup butter or margarine, room temperature

1 cup fresh bread crumbs

2 cloves garlic, minced

3 tablespoons finely minced onion

½ cup chopped parsley

¼ cup white wine or sherry

Juice from ½ lemon

¼ teaspoon salt

⅛ teaspoon pepper

Serves 6.

To prepare Garlic Butter, mix together butter, crumbs, garlic, onion, parsley, wine, lemon juice, salt and pepper. Form into a roll and wrap in waxed paper. Chill until firm. Can be made a day in advance.

Preheat oven to 350 degrees.

Melt butter in large skillet over medium heat. Add onion and sauté until soft and transparent. Add scallops and mushrooms. Sauté briefly until scallops are barely done. Drain liquid.

Place rice in a greased casserole. Arrange broccoli and scallop mixture on top.

Slice Garlic Butter in ¼ - ½ inch slices and lay on top of casserole.

Bake 10-15 minutes until Garlic Butter is bubbly.

BAYVIEW SHRIMP AND SCALLOPS

Elegant served in a scallop shell

2 cups scallops

2 cups water

⅓ cup dry white wine (optional)

1½ cups small cooked shrimp

2 cups cooked orzo or rice

SAUCE

¼ cup margarine

¼ cup flour

¼ teaspoon salt

⅛ teaspoon pepper

2 cups milk

½ cup chopped celery

½ cup chopped onion

2 teaspoons margarine

1 teaspoon Worcestershire
   sauce

½ cup grated Swiss or Monterey
   Jack cheese

⅓ cup poaching liquid from
   scallops

1 tablespoon minced parsley

CRUMB TOPPING

1 cup dry bread crumbs

2 tablespoons melted margarine

¼ cup freshly grated Parmesan
   cheese

Serves 6.

Place scallops in a saucepan. Add water and white wine. Bring barely to a boil. Remove from heat and let stand until scallops are opaque. Drain liquid, saving some to add to the sauce.

Prepare sauce. Melt margarine. Stir in flour, salt and pepper. Cook and stir for 2 minutes. Gradually add milk and heat, stirring frequently. While sauce is cooking, sauté celery and onions in margarine to soften. Add sautéed celery, onion, Worcestershire sauce, cheese, scallop liquid and parsley to thickened sauce. Add scallops and shrimp.

Preheat oven to 350 degrees.

In greased individual ramekins or a casserole dish, place a layer of rice or orzo. Pour seafood sauce on top. Add Crumb Topping.

Bake 20-30 minutes or until bubbly.

To prepare Crumb Topping, combine bread crumbs and margarine. Add Parmesan cheese and mix well.

Gearhart Clam Bake with Shrimp Sauce

No digging required

6 eggs

1½ cups milk

1 teaspoon salt

¼ teaspoon black pepper

2 tablespoons Worcestershire
sauce

3½ cups cooked rice

¾ cup chopped green onion

1 (4-ounce) can chopped
pimiento

½ cup minced fresh parsley

2½ cups grated sharp cheddar
cheese

2 cups (four 7-ounce cans)
minced clams, drained

Shrimp Sauce

3 tablespoons margarine

3 tablespoons flour

½ cup chicken broth

½ cup milk

½ cup sour cream

1 teaspoon lemon juice

¼ teaspoon curry powder

1 cup small cooked shrimp

Serves 12.

Preheat oven to 325 degrees.

Beat eggs. Add milk, salt, pepper and Worcestershire sauce and blend well. Stir in rice, green onion, pimiento and parsley. Add cheese and clams, mixing well.

Spread in a buttered 9 by 13-inch baking pan. Bake 50-60 minutes.

Cut into squares and serve with Shrimp Sauce.

To prepare Shrimp Sauce, melt margarine in a saucepan. Add flour, cook and stir for 2 minutes over low heat. Add chicken broth and milk. Heat, stirring constantly, until sauce thickens. Add sour cream, lemon juice and curry powder. Stir and remove from heat.

Just before serving, add shrimp and reheat, carefully.

You may add more curry powder if desired.

Fresh Tomato Basil Tart

A good reason for planting that garden — delicious!

2 cups flour

¼ teaspoon salt

2 tablespoons sugar

4 teaspoons baking powder

⅓ cup vegetable shortening

¾ cup buttermilk

Filling

5 - 6 medium tomatoes, peeled
    and diced in 1-inch cubes

½ teaspoon salt

2 teaspoons chopped fresh basil
    or ½ teaspoon dried basil

Topping

1 cup mayonnaise

1 cup grated Swiss cheese

1 cup grated sharp cheddar
    cheese

2 tablespoons Parmesan cheese

Serves 6.

Preheat oven to 450 degrees.

Combine flour, salt, sugar and baking powder. Cut shortening into flour mixture. Add buttermilk and stir with a fork until just barely mixed. Cover and let rest for half an hour.

Combine tomatoes, salt and basil for filling. In a separate bowl, combine mayonnaise and cheese for topping.

To assemble, use 6 (10-ounce) greased individual soufflé dishes and divide dough equally among the dishes. Press dough across the bottom and up the sides. Bake crusts for 8 minutes or until golden brown. Remove dishes and lower heat to 400 degrees.

Divide tomato filling among dishes and mound about ½ cup topping on each. Bake for about 15 minutes until bubbly and browned.

GARDEN QUICHE

Compliment this with melon slices

3 tablespoons butter

1 large onion, chopped

¼ pound mushrooms, sliced

8 ounces chopped frozen spinach, thawed

4 eggs, beaten

2 cups half and half

2 tablespoons flour

¼ teaspoon nutmeg

¼ teaspoon cayenne pepper

¼ teaspoon white pepper

¼ teaspoon salt

2 cups grated Swiss or cheddar cheese or combination of both

¼ cup grated Parmesan cheese

1 (10-inch) unbaked pie crust

1 egg white, slightly beaten

Serves 8.

Preheat oven to 350 degrees.

Melt butter, add onion, mushrooms and sauté until onion is translucent.

Squeeze spinach dry.

Combine beaten eggs, half and half, flour, nutmeg, cayenne, white pepper and salt. Add onion, mushrooms and spinach. Mix gently. Add cheeses. Brush pie crust with egg white.

Pour combined ingredients into crust. Bake 35-45 minutes or until a knife inserted comes out clean. Let cool 5-10 minutes before cutting.

Cheese Cannelloni with Italian Sauce

Egg roll wrappers make this light and easy

Sauce

2 tablespoons butter or margarine

1 onion, chopped

1 clove garlic, crushed

½ teaspoon salt

½ teaspoon pepper

¼ teaspoon basil

1 chicken bouillon cube

1 (28-ounce) can Italian plum tomatoes

Filling

3 eggs

2 tablespoons chopped parsley

¼ teaspoon salt

¼ teaspoon pepper

8 ounces ricotta cheese

¾ cup Parmesan cheese

¼ cup grated Romano cheese

½ pound mozzarella cheese, grated

½ pound provolone cheese, grated

8 - 10 egg roll wrappers

Serves 6-8.

Preheat oven to 350 degrees.

Melt butter in large saucepan over medium heat. Add onion and garlic and sauté for 1 minute. Add salt, pepper, basil, bouillon cube and tomatoes with juice. Cook, stirring occasionally, for 15-20 minutes until thickened. Puree in food processor or blender. Set aside.

Beat eggs in large bowl. Add parsley, salt and pepper, mixing well. Add the cheeses and stir until well combined.

Spread ½ cup sauce on bottom of 9 by 13-inch baking dish. Place about 3 tablespoons of cheese filling onto each egg roll wrapper. Roll and place seam side down in dish. Pour remaining sauce over rolls. Bake 20-30 minutes or until sauce is bubbly.

STUFFED JUMBO PASTA SHELLS WITH ITALIAN SAUCES

Dramatic and delicious with red and white sauces

FILLING

¾ cup finely chopped onion

1 clove garlic, minced

3 tablespoons butter or margarine

1 (10-ounce) package frozen spinach, thawed and pressed dry

2 eggs

½ teaspoon oregano

¼ teaspoon salt

¼ teaspoon black pepper

2 cups ricotta cheese

¼ cup grated Parmesan cheese

1 tablespoon chopped parsley

16 - 18 jumbo-sized pasta shells or egg roll wrappers

Chopped parsley for garnish

ITALIAN RED SAUCE

2 tablespoons butter or margarine

¾ cup chopped onion

1 clove garlic, minced

1 (28-ounce) can Italian plum tomatoes with juice, blended in food processor

½ teaspoon salt

½ teaspoon pepper

1 teaspoon dried basil

1 teaspoon chicken-flavored seasoning

Serves 8.

Preheat oven to 350 degrees.

To make filling, sauté onions and garlic in butter until onion is translucent. Beat eggs and add oregano, salt and pepper. Place ricotta cheese in a large bowl. Gradually add egg mixture to ricotta, mixing well. Combine Parmesan cheese and parsley and add to ricotta mixture. Add sautéed onion and garlic. Gradually add spinach. Fill cooked pasta shells or egg roll wrappers.

To prepare Italian Red Sauce, sauté onions and garlic in butter until translucent. Add tomatoes and seasoning. Simmer over low heat, stirring occasionally until thickened.

To prepare Béchamel Sauce, melt butter or margarine in a saucepan. Stir in flour, salt. and cook for 2 minutes. Add half and half, milk and seasonings. Heat, stirring constantly, until thickened. Stir in wine.

Arrange shells or wrappers in a 9 by 13-inch baking pan or 8 individual ramekins. Carefully spoon Italian Red Sauce over half the shells, then spoon Béchamel Sauce over the rest. Heat 15-20 minutes. Sprinkle with chopped fresh parsley. Each serving consists of one white and one red sauced pasta.

STUFFED JUMBO PASTA SHELLS WITH ITALIAN SAUCES

BÉCHAMEL SAUCE

¼ cup butter or margarine

¼ cup flour

1 cup half and half

¾ cup milk

¼ teaspoon salt

½ teaspoon chicken-flavored seasoning

⅛ teaspoon pepper

⅛ teaspoon powdered thyme

¼ cup dry white wine

FLORENTINE CREPES WITH MUSHROOM SAUCE

Rich and worth the effort

2 tablespoons butter

1 cup chopped onion

1 ½ tablespoons flour

⅔ cup half and half

½ teaspoon salt

½ teaspoon lemon juice

2 (10-ounce) packages of frozen chopped spinach, thawed and pressed dry

12 - 16 (6-inch) crepes

2 cups grated Swiss cheese

Paprika

SAUCE

1 cup sliced fresh mushrooms

2 tablespoons butter

3 tablespoons flour

1 cup chicken broth

½ cup sour cream

⅛ teaspoon white pepper

Serves 6-8.

Preheat oven to 350 degrees.

Grease a 9 by 13-inch baking pan.

Sauté onion in butter. Sprinkle flour over onion. Stir and cook for 2-3 minutes. Add half and half, salt and lemon juice. Heat, stirring, 3-5 minutes until thickened. Remove from heat. Gradually stir in spinach.

Allowing two crepes per serving, put a scant ¼ cup filling in each crepe. Add 2 tablespoons cheese. Roll crepes and place seam down in baking dish.

Prepare sauce: melt butter and sauté mushrooms. Add flour and mix well. Add broth, sour cream and pepper. Heat, stirring often, until thickened.

Pour sauce over center of crepes, leaving tips showing. Sprinkle with paprika.

Bake for 20-25 minutes or until hot and bubbly.

NOTE: See BASIC CREPE RECIPE page 131.

BROCCOLI AND CHEESE STRATA

Make ahead for an easy brunch. Add fresh fruit and your favorite muffin.

12 - 16 slices white bread, crusts removed

½ pound cheddar cheese, grated

1 (10-ounce) package frozen chopped broccoli, thawed and drained

¼ cup finely chopped onion

5 eggs, lightly beaten

2½ cups milk

½ teaspoon salt

¼ teaspoon dry mustard

1 cup grated Monterey Jack or Swiss cheese

Paprika

Serves 10-12.

Place half of the bread in a buttered 9 by 13-inch pan making one solid layer. Spread cheddar cheese on top of bread. Layer broccoli over cheese, then add onion. Top with a layer of remaining bread.

Combine eggs, milk, salt and mustard. Pour over casserole. Cover and refrigerate 6 hours or overnight.

Preheat oven to 325 degrees.

Bake 50-55 minutes. Sprinkle with Monterey Jack or Swiss cheese and paprika. Bake 5 more minutes. Let stand 10 minutes before serving.

As a variation, 2 cups chopped ham or one half pound crisply fried and crumbled bacon may be added.

CHEESE PUFF

An all-time favorite. Try it for brunch.

FILLING

2 cups grated sharp cheddar cheese

2 cups grated Monterey Jack cheese

1 medium tomato, seeded and chopped

1 (4-ounce) can diced green chiles

¼ cup sliced black olives, drained

1 tablespoon flour

TOPPING

3 eggs, separated

3 tablespoons flour

⅓ cup evaporated milk

¼ teaspoon salt

¼ teaspoon oregano

⅛ teaspoon ground cumin

⅛ teaspoon pepper

⅛ teaspoon cream of tartar

Serves 6-8.

Preheat oven to 350 degrees.

Combine first 5 filling ingredients. Toss with flour. May be refrigerated at this point.

To prepare topping, beat egg yolks. Gradually blend in flour and milk. Add salt, oregano, cumin and pepper. Mix well. Beat egg whites until foamy. Add cream of tartar and beat until stiff. Fold yolk mixture into whites.

Place cheese-filling mixture in greased shallow 9 by 13-inch baking pan. Spoon topping over cheese mixture.

Bake 20-30 minutes or until egg topping is puffed and browned. Serve immediately.

As a variation, line a pan with cooked brown and wild rice before adding filling and topping.

BASIC CREPE RECIPE

1 cup flour

1½ cups milk

2 eggs

1 tablespoon cooking oil

¼ teaspoon salt

Makes 16-18.

Combine flour, milk, eggs, oil and salt in a bowl. Beat until blended. May be made in a blender.

Heat (on medium) a lightly greased 6-inch skillet. Remove from heat. Spoon 2 tablespoons of batter into skillet. Lift and tilt skillet to spread batter evenly. Return to heat and brown on one side only. Remove by inverting pan over paper toweling.

Crepes may be made ahead and frozen. Stack crepes between two layers of waxed paper then seal in a moisture-proof bag and place in freezer.

Side Dishes

Albertina's is managed by a group of volunteers called the Steering Committee. This Committee, which meets monthly, coordinates the daily operation of the restaurant, provides fiscal leadership to insure business profitability, strives to maintain the gracious image of Albertina's and is responsible for recruitment and training of volunteer personnel and professional staff.

MUSTARD-PICKLED BEANS

A tangy favorite

1 cup sugar

½ cup cider vinegar

3 tablespoons prepared mustard

½ teaspoon instant minced
   onion

¼ teaspoon salt

1 (1-pound) can whole green
   beans, drained

Serves 6.

Combine sugar, vinegar, mustard, minced onion and salt. Bring to a boil, stirring, to dissolve sugar. Add green beans. Simmer, uncovered, for 5 minutes. Cool. Store in a non-metallic bowl. Cover and refrigerate overnight.

CARDAMOM CARROTS

The aroma of the freshly ground cardamom is special. Serve with
CHICKEN ZORBA.

8 medium carrots

1 small red pepper, seeded

¼ cup butter

2 tablespoons honey

1 teaspoon grated lemon rind

2 tablespoons fresh lemon juice

2 tablespoons orange juice

2 tablespoons dry vermouth

⅜ teaspoon freshly ground
   cardamom

⅛ teaspoon salt

⅛ teaspoon pepper

Serves 8.

Wash, peel and cut carrots into diagonal chunks about ½ inch thick. Boil in a small quantity of water for approximately 4 minutes or until crisply done. Immediately plunge into ice water and drain. Set aside.

Cut red pepper into julienne strips and set aside.

To prepare the sauce, combine the next 9 ingredients and bring to a boil. Add the carrots and heat through. Add the red pepper strips just before serving.

CARROT TIMBALE

A colorful partner to any meat entrée

2 pounds carrots

3 cups water

¾ teaspoon salt

2 large eggs, beaten

2 cups grated sharp cheddar
   cheese

¼ teaspoon salt

¼ teaspoon white pepper

⅓ cup dry bread crumbs
   (optional)

Parsley, chopped

Serves 8-10.

Preheat oven to 350 degrees.

Peel carrots, cut in pieces and simmer in salted water until tender. Drain and discard water. Mash carrots. (Can be done in processor.)

Combine mashed carrots with beaten eggs, cheese, salt and pepper.

Pour into greased 8- by 11-inch baking dish. If desired, may sprinkle with bread crumbs. Bake, uncovered, 20-30 minutes until firm but not browned. Sprinkle with fresh chopped parsley before serving.

BAKED TOMATOES PROVENCE

Adds a colorful spot on a plate

2 medium tomatoes

½ teaspoon Herbes de Provence

Parsley sprigs

Serves 4.

Preheat oven to 350 degrees.

Remove stem area from tomatoes. Cut in halves crosswise. Place cut edge up in small baking pan. Sprinkle with Herbes de Provence. Bake for 15 minutes. Garnish with parsley sprigs.

As a variation, you may substitute Italian seasonings for Herbes de Provence or sprinkle a scant teaspoon of Parmesan cheese on each tomato half before baking.

Pea Salad with Sunflower Seeds

Great garnish or salad

1 (10-ounce) package frozen peas, thawed

¼ cup chopped green onions

¼ cup finely chopped celery

¼ cup seasoned rice vinegar

¼ cup roasted sunflower seeds

Lettuce

Serves 6-8 as a garnish.

Combine peas, onions and celery. Add seasoned rice vinegar about ½ hour before serving. Stir several times.

At serving time, drain peas. Add sunflower seeds and serve in a lettuce cup. (You may sprinkle sunflower seeds over the top instead of mixing them into the salad.)

Zucchini Slaw

4 medium zucchini, grated

2 green onions

1 small red pepper, seeded

1 small green pepper, seeded

1 rib of celery

⅓ cup sugar

⅓ cup white wine vinegar

3 tablespoons salad oil

½ teaspoon salt

Serves 8-12.

Using grater blade, grate zucchini in food processor. Remove zucchini to bowl.

Change to steel blade.

Cut onions and celery in one inch lengths. Cut peppers in one inch squares. Put onion, celery and peppers in food processor and pulse several times until chopped. Add to zucchini.

Mix sugar, vinegar, oil and salt until well blended. Pour over vegetables and mix well. Chill at least 1 hour and up to 2 days. Drain at serving time. Use as a salad or as a garnish.

BAKED CRANBERRY RELISH

A perfect compliment to Thanksgiving dinner

1 quart fresh cranberries,
    washed

2 cups sugar

¼ cup water

1 teaspoon cinnamon

½ cup broken walnuts or pecans

Serves 16.

Preheat oven to 300 degrees.

Combine berries, sugar and water. Place in ungreased 1½-quart baking dish. Cover. Bake for 30 minutes. Stir. Increase oven temperature to 350 degrees. Sprinkle cinnamon over berries and bake 5-15 more minutes until the berries are clear but still whole. Sprinkle nuts on top and serve warm.

BRANDIED CRANBERRIES

May be used to fill peach halves

4 cups fresh cranberries,
    washed

2 cups sugar

½ cup brandy

Serves 16.

Preheat oven to 300 degrees.

Combine cranberries, sugar and brandy. Mix well. Place in oiled 9- by 13-inch baking dish and cover with foil. Bake at 300 degrees for 30-45 minutes, stirring 2-3 times. Remove from oven when berries are soft but still plump.

Serve in small glass cups or dishes.

CRANBERRY BUTTER

A pretty hostess gift for the holidays

1 cup fresh cranberries, washed

Rind of ¼ of an orange

½ cup sugar

1 pound softened butter

Makes 3 cups.

Grind cranberries and orange rind in a processor. Transfer to a glass bowl. Add sugar and mix well. Allow mixture to sit 1-2 days in refrigerator.

Beat butter with an electric mixer until it is light and fluffy. Gradually add cranberry mixture, beating well between additions. Form in balls or fill small individual cups.

CRYSTAL DILL PICKLES

Add something homemade to a relish tray

1 (2-quart) jar prepared dill pickles, drained

4 small onions, sliced ¼ inch thick

2½ cups sugar

1½ cups cider vinegar

½ cup water

2 large cinnamon sticks

Makes 2 quarts.

Slice dill pickles in ½-inch rounds. Separate onion slices in rings. Return pickle rounds to jar in alternating layers with onion rings.

Heat sugar, vinegar and water in a saucepan until sugar dissolves. Pour syrup over pickles and onions. Add cinnamon sticks to jar and replace top. Refrigerate at least 2 days before serving.

CONFETTI RICE

Colorful and tasty

4 cups cooked rice

½ cup finely chopped uncooked
   carrots

½ cup finely chopped celery

⅓ cup chopped green onions

2 tablespoons chopped fresh
   parsley

Serves 8.

Combine cooked rice, carrots, celery and onions. Reheat rice just enough to warm, being careful not to cook vegetables. Add parsley just before serving.

LEMON PILAF

Particularly nice with chicken

2 tablespoons butter

1 tablespoon minced onion

1 cup long-grain white rice (not
   quick cooking)

1½ cups chicken broth

¼ cup lemon juice

Rind of 1 lemon, finely grated

2 tablespoons currants

¼ cup toasted slivered almonds

Serves 8.

In a 2-quart saucepan, melt butter and sauté onion until transparent. Add raw rice and stir to coat grains with butter. Stir in chicken broth, lemon juice and lemon rind. Bring to a boil, then immediately lower heat and simmer for 15-20 minutes, covered. When almost all the liquid is absorbed, stir in currants. Continue simmering, covered, until all liquid is absorbed. Remove from heat and add almonds just before serving.

FRUITED RICE

Very unique. Serve with ALSACE CHICKEN.

1 cup long-grain rice

2 tablespoons butter

½ teaspoon curry powder

2 cups chicken broth

2 bananas, sliced

2 tablespoons orange juice

½ cup raisins

½ cup toasted slivered almonds

Serves 8-10.

Combine rice, butter, curry powder and chicken broth. Simmer over low heat until liquid is absorbed and rice is tender.

Toss bananas with orange juice to prevent discoloring. Add bananas, raisins and almonds to rice. Toss to combine. Warm in microwave oven.

BARLEY AND SUNFLOWER SEED PILAF

1 cup pearl barley

2 tablespoons butter

⅓ cup sunflower seeds

1 cup chopped green onions

¼ teaspoon salt

¼ teaspoon pepper

3½ cups chicken broth

½ cup chopped fresh parsley

Serves 8-10.

Preheat oven to 350 degrees.

Rinse barley in warm water and drain. Melt butter and sauté onions, barley and sunflower seeds. Stir in salt and pepper. Spoon into a buttered 2-quart casserole. Heat broth to boiling and pour over barley mixture. Stir to blend well. Cover and bake for 1 hour and 10 minutes or until all liquid is absorbed. Add parsley just before serving.

WILD RICE AND ORZO WITH WALNUTS

Excellent nutty flavor

1 ½ cups wild rice

6 cups water

1 teaspoon salt

6 tablespoons walnut oil or olive oil

1 pound orzo

3 tablespoons fresh lemon juice

Salt and pepper

⅔ cup finely chopped green onions

1 cup chopped toasted walnuts

Serves 12.

In a large saucepan, combine rice with water and salt. Simmer, covered, until tender, 40 to 45 minutes. Drain rice well and transfer to a large bowl. Toss rice with 2 tablespoons oil.

In a saucepan of boiling salted water, cook orzo until al dente. Rinse under cold water and drain well. to rice mixture add orzo with remaining 4 tablespoons oil, lemon juice and salt and pepper, to taste. Toss well. Mixture may be prepared to this point one day ahead. Cover and chill.

Just before serving, stir in green onions and walnuts and season with additional lemon juice and salt and pepper, if needed. Serve warm or at room temperature.

Acini de Pepe Pasta

A flavorful accompaniment to beef or poultry

1 cup Acini de Pepe pasta

1 teaspoon chicken base or
    bouillon

¼ cup butter

½ cup chopped onions

½ cup minced mushrooms

½ teaspoon garlic salt

½ cup fresh parsley, chopped

Serves 4-6.

Cook pasta according to directions on package. Drain well and rinse in cold water.

Melt butter and sauté onions and mushrooms. Add garlic salt and chicken base or bouillon. Mix sautéed vegetables and pasta. Add parsley just before serving. May be prepared in advance and reheated.

Rosa Marina (Orzo) Pasta

For a change, try substituting this for noodles

1 cup orzo

2 quarts boiling salted water

¼ cup minced yellow onion

¼ cup butter

1 teaspoon chicken base or
    bouillon

½ teaspoon garlic salt

¼ cup minced fresh parsley

Serves 4-6.

Add pasta to boiling water and simmer for 10-15 minutes or until tender. Drain in a sieve and rinse with cold water. Set aside.

Heat butter in a small skillet. Add onions and sauté until they are transparent. Add chicken base or bouillon and garlic salt. Mix well. Add pasta and heat through. Stir in parsley.

Breads & Muffins

Albertina's opened in May 1981, the culmination of a dream and several years of hard work by dedicated volunteers. It is a very special restaurant, unique in Oregon, open to the public for lunch five days a week and staffed and managed by volunteers. A private dining room is available to groups of eight to thirty for luncheon meetings, card parties, celebrations and other special events.

KERR ROLLS

These rolls were first made in the Old Kerr Nursery. They continue to be loved by all. An easy yeast-bread recipe.

½ cup milk

½ cup melted butter

¼ cup sugar

½ teaspoon salt

1 package dry yeast

3 tablespoons lukewarm water

2 eggs, beaten

3 - 3½ cups flour

Makes 30 rolls.

Heat milk to lukewarm. Add melted butter, sugar and salt. Stir and set aside. Combine yeast and lukewarm water. Let stand 5 minutes, then add yeast mixture to lukewarm milk and mix well. Add beaten eggs and mix flour in gradually until dough can be kneaded. (Do not try to work in too much flour.) Knead dough for 5 minutes. Place in greased bowl, cover tightly, and refrigerate overnight.

To prepare rolls to bake, divide dough into 3 parts. Roll each part into a circle. Cut 10 pie-shaped pieces from each circle. Roll from wide edge to point of each wedge. Place point down on greased baking sheets. Cover and let rise, in a warm place until doubled in size.

Bake in preheated 400 degree oven for 10 minutes or until golden brown.

To make bread sticks, divide dough in halves and roll each half in an 8- by 10-inch rectangle. Cut dough in halves so that there are two (8- by 5-inch) pieces of dough. Cut in 1-inch strips. Twist and place on greased baking sheets. You may brush with beaten egg and water and sprinkle with sesame seeds or poppy seeds. Let rise and bake according to main recipe instructions.

LEMON PUFF YEAST ROLLS

1 package dry yeast

¼ cup lukewarm water

¾ cup milk

6 tablespoons sugar

¾ teaspoon salt

⅓ cup shortening

1 tablespoon grated lemon peel

1 teaspoon lemon juice

2 eggs, beaten

3 cups all-purpose flour

TOPPING

2 tablespoons sugar

1 teaspoon cinnamon

Makes 18 muffin-size rolls.

Soften the dry yeast in ¼ cup lukewarm water. Scald the milk and add sugar, salt, shortening, lemon peel and lemon juice. Cool to lukewarm. Add beaten eggs and milk to yeast mixture and mix well.

Add flour, 1 cup at a time, beating until smooth after each addition. Cover and let rise until doubled in size. Stir dough down.

Fill greased muffin pans half full. (May refrigerate at this time.)

When ready to bake, sprinkle ¼ teaspoon topping on each roll. Cover and let rise in a warm place until doubled in size.

Bake at 375 degrees for 15-20 minutes.

HEARTY BROWN BREAD

An excellent accompaniment to JARLSBERG VEGETABLE SOUP

3 cups whole-wheat flour

1¼ teaspoons baking soda

1 teaspoon salt

2 cups buttermilk (or sour milk)

½ cup light molasses

Makes 1 loaf of bread.

Preheat oven to 300 degrees.

Sift together dry ingredients. Stir in milk and molasses. Put in well-greased 9 by 5-inch bread pan.

Bake for 1 hour or until center tests done. Cool slightly and slice.

KONA INN BANANA BREAD

Beyond banana bread!

2 cups sugar

1 cup softened butter

6 very ripe (black) bananas, mashed (approximately 3 cups)

4 eggs, well beaten

2½ cups cake flour

2 teaspoons baking soda

1 teaspoon salt

Makes 2 loaves.

Preheat oven to 350 degrees.

Cream together sugar and butter until light and fluffy. Add bananas and eggs, beating until well blended.

Sift dry ingredients together 3 times.

Blend with banana mixture, but do not over mix. Pour into 2 greased and floured (5 by 9-inch) loaf pans.

Bake for 45-60 minutes, until firm in center and the edges begin to separate from pan.

Cool on a rack for 10 minutes before removing from the pan. After completely cooled, cut into thin slices.

Loaf freezes beautifully.

For full flavor, bananas should be ripened until they are black.

STRAWBERRY BREAD

A year round treat

3 cups flour

1 teaspoon baking soda

1 teaspoon salt

1 tablespoon cinnamon

2 cups sugar

4 eggs, beaten

2 cups frozen strawberries, thawed (includes juice)

1½ cups oil

1¼ cups chopped pecans

Makes 2 loaves.

Preheat oven to 325 degrees.

Grease and flour two 9 x 5 loaf pans.

Sift the dry ingredients together. In a separate bowl, combine eggs, strawberries and oil. Mix all ingredients and stir in pecans.

Divide the mixture evenly between the pans and bake for 1 hour or until bread tests done. Cool in pans for 10 minutes then remove loaves and cool completely on racks.

CHEDDAR DROP BISCUITS

Great with soup or salad

1 cup sifted flour

1½ teaspoons baking powder

¼ teaspoon salt

2 tablespoons cold butter, cut into bits

1½ cups grated cheddar cheese

½ cup milk

Makes 10-12 medium biscuits.

Preheat oven to 400 degrees.

Sift together flour, baking powder and salt. Add bits of butter and cheese to flour mixture. (A food processor could be used to do this.) Stir in milk to form a soft sticky dough. Drop by rounded spoonfuls onto greased baking sheet.

Bake 12-15 minutes or until pale golden brown.

NO-FAIL BISCUITS

Amazingly light!

2 cups sifted flour

1 tablespoon sugar

4 teaspoons baking powder

½ teaspoon salt

½ cup shortening

1 egg, beaten

⅔ cup milk

Makes 15 medium biscuits.

Preheat oven to 450 degrees.

Sift dry ingredients, cutting in shortening until it resembles coarse crumbs.

Combine egg and milk. Add all at once to flour mixture. Stir with a fork until a soft mass is formed.

Turn onto floured surface and knead gently 15-20 strokes. Roll to ¾-inch thickness and cut in 2-inch squares or rounds. Place on ungreased baking sheet 1 inch apart. (May refrigerate at this point.)

Bake for 10-14 minutes.

For drop biscuits, increase milk to ¾ cup and omit kneading. Drop onto baking sheet.

PUFF PASTRY TWISTS

Easy and elegant

1 sheet frozen puff pastry

1 egg

1 tablespoon water

3 tablespoons grated Parmesan
   cheese

Poppy seeds

Makes about 28 twists.

Preheat oven to 400 degrees.

Thaw puff pastry 20 minutes. Beat egg lightly with water and set aside.

On a lightly floured surface, roll sheet to a 10 by 14-inch rectangle. Cut in halves lengthwise to make 2 rectangles. Brush each rectangle with egg mixture; sprinkle one with Parmesan cheese and the other with poppy seeds.

Lay one rectangle directly over the other, making sure the egg-brushed sides are touching. Roll very gently with a rolling pin to make pastry stick together. Brush with more egg and sprinkle with poppy seeds.

Cut pastry crosswise into ½-inch strips. Twist strips into corkscrew shapes and put on ungreased baking sheet. Bake for 10-12 minutes, or until puffed and golden brown.

Variations: In place of Parmesan cheese and poppy seeds, substitute shredded cheddar cheese and sesame seeds, or shredded fontina cheese and cayenne pepper. Or, spread the pastry with Roka Bleu Cheese Spread, eliminating the egg wash. For salt sticks, cut a single layer of pastry into strips, brush with egg, and sprinkle with coarse salt.

CHEESE TWISTS

These will disappear fast!

1 egg

1 tablespoon water

2 sheets puff pastry

1 cup grated sharp cheddar cheese

1/8 teaspoon cayenne pepper

1/2 cup grated Parmesan cheese

Makes 48 twists.

Preheat oven to 375 degrees.

Beat egg and water together. Brush one pastry sheet with egg wash. Sprinkle cheddar cheese on pastry sheet. Mix cayenne and Parmesan cheese together and sprinkle half of mixture on the pastry sheet.

Cover with second sheet of pastry. With rolling pin, roll pastry sheets until doubled in size. Brush top sheet with egg wash and sprinkle with remaining cayenne and Parmesan mixture.

Cut into 3/4 by 6-inch strips or desired length and twist 2-3 times loosely. Place on parchment-lined or greased cookie sheet.

Bake for 12-15 minutes or until puffed and golden brown. Remove immediately.

CELERY SEED BAGUETTE

1 baguette

1 cup softened butter

1/2 teaspoon celery seeds

1/4 teaspoon paprika

Preheat oven to 350 degrees.

Cut baguette lengthwise and lay on ungreased baking sheet, cut side up.

Mix butter, celery seeds and paprika. Spread on top of cut bread.

Bake for 5-10 minutes or until topping is melted and bread is toasted on edges. Cut wide slices.

SAVORY TOAST

The name says it all

16 thin slices white bread

1 cup butter, softened

½ teaspoon thyme

¼ teaspoon savory

¼ teaspoon paprika

Makes 32 triangles.

Preheat oven to 350 degrees.

Remove crusts from bread slices and cut into triangles.

Mix butter with seasonings. Spread top of each slice with seasoned butter.

Place on ungreased baking sheet and bake until golden brown. Can be made ahead and reheated before serving.

PANTRY CHEESE BREAD

An old Portland favorite

½ pound margarine, softened

¼ pound sharp cheddar cheese, grated

½ cup grated Romano or Parmesan cheese

¼ teaspoon paprika

⅛ teaspoon garlic powder

½ teaspoon Worcestershire sauce

1 - 2 loaves French bread

Preheat oven to 350 degrees.

Bring margarine to room temperature. (Do not melt.)

Combine cheeses, paprika and garlic powder. Add this mixture to the margarine and whip together. Stir in the Worcestershire sauce.

Spread on split or sliced French bread.

Bake on ungreased baking sheets until spread has melted into bread or bread is slightly toasted, whichever is your preference.

SCONES

Light, quick and tasty

2 cups flour

2¼ teaspoons baking powder

2 tablespoons sugar

¼ teaspoon salt

¼ cup cold butter

½ cup currants

2 eggs, beaten

⅓ cup whipping cream

1 egg, beaten

Sugar

SWISS HONEY BUTTER

½ cup soft butter

⅓ cup whipping cream

¼ cup honey

Makes 12 to 15 scones.

Preheat oven to 400 degrees.

Sift dry ingredients into food processor. Add butter in chunks and process until fine. Transfer to a large bowl and add currants. Set aside.

Combine 2 eggs and cream, mix thoroughly. Add to dry ingredients. Mix only until cream is absorbed. Knead lightly.

Roll out 1-inch thick and cut in desired shapes. Place on ungreased baking sheet. Brush with a little beaten egg and sprinkle lightly with sugar.

Bake for about 10 minutes.

Serve with Swiss Honey Butter.

To prepare Swiss Honey Butter, cream butter and slowly add cream and honey. Beat until smooth and thick.

PITA CRISPS

So easy, so delicious!

8 pita bread rounds
½ - ¾ cup melted butter

Makes 64 pita crisps.

Preheat oven to 350 degrees.

Cut each pita bread into quarters. Gently separate each piece, making 2 parts or pieces.

Brush insides of each piece with melted butter. Place buttered side up on ungreased baking sheets.

Bake for 10-15 minutes or until crisp and golden brown.

Variation: Parmesan Dill Crisps — Before baking, sprinkle buttered pita pieces with Parmesan cheese and dill weed.

BRAN APPLE MUFFINS

Apples make these moist

2½ cups 40% Bran Flakes
1 cup milk
⅔ cup margarine, softened
¾ cup sugar
1 egg, beaten
1½ cups sifted flour
1 tablespoon baking powder
1 teaspoon cinnamon
¼ teaspoon nutmeg
½ teaspoon salt
1 cup unpeeled grated apple

Makes 18 muffins.

Preheat oven to 400 degrees.

Combine cereal and milk and let stand until softened.

Cream margarine and sugar. Blend in cereal mixture. Add beaten egg.

Add remaining dry ingredients to cereal mixture and stir just until moistened. Stir in apple.

Spoon into greased muffin tin, filling each cup ⅔ full.

Bake for 15-20 minutes.

BLUEBERRY STREUSEL MUFFINS

The whole-wheat flour and streusel topping make these doubly delicious

1 cup sifted white flour

½ cup sifted whole-wheat flour

2 teaspoons baking powder

½ teaspoon baking soda

¼ teaspoon salt

¾ cup sugar

1 ½ cups fresh or frozen blueberries

⅔ cup buttermilk

½ cup butter, melted and cooled

2 large eggs, beaten

1 teaspoon vanilla

STREUSEL TOPPING

¼ cup sugar

3 tablespoons flour

½ teaspoon cinnamon

1 tablespoon cold butter, in pieces

Makes 18 medium muffins.

Preheat oven to 375 degrees.

Mix together 2 kinds of flour, baking powder, baking soda, salt and sugar. Add berries to dry ingredients.

Combine buttermilk, butter, eggs and vanilla and add to flour mixture. Mix just until flour disappears.

To make topping, combine sugar, flour and cinnamon; cut in butter.

Fill greased muffin tin ⅔ full and sprinkle streusel topping on each muffin.

Bake for about 15 minutes or until firm to the touch and lightly browned.

Bran Muffins

An old standby

3¾ cups All Bran
2 cups 100% bran
1 teaspoon salt
2 cups boiling water
3¾ cups buttermilk
1 cup shortening
3 cups sugar
6 eggs
5 cups flour
5 teaspoons baking soda

Makes 60 muffins.

Preheat oven to 375 degrees.

In a large container combine both brans and salt. Add water and buttermilk to bran mixture and cool.

Cream shortening and sugar. Beat eggs into shortening mixture and add bran mixture.

Sift flour and baking soda together and add to bran mixture. Can be stored in refrigerator at this point, for 2-3 weeks.

Do not stir after refrigeration. Spoon into greased muffin tin, filling ⅔ full.

Bake for 20-25 minutes.

BROWN SUGAR MUFFINS

1 cup brown sugar

½ cup butter, softened

1 egg, beaten

1 cup milk

2 cups sifted flour

½ teaspoon salt

½ teaspoon baking soda

1 teaspoon baking powder

½ cup chopped nuts

½ teaspoon vanilla

Makes about 18 medium muffins

Preheat oven to 400 degrees.

Cream sugar and butter. Add egg and milk and stir well.

Combine flour, salt, baking soda and baking powder. Add to milk mixture.

Stir in nuts and vanilla.

Fill greased muffin tins ⅔ full.

Bake for about 15 minutes or until firm to the touch.

COUNTRY CORN MUFFINS

1 ¼ cups yellow cornmeal

1 cup unsifted flour

¼ cup sugar

¼ cup firmly packed, light-brown sugar

1 teaspoon baking soda

¼ teaspoon salt

1 egg

1 cup buttermilk

⅔ cup corn oil

Makes 12-15 medium-sized muffins.

Preheat oven to 425 degrees.

With a fork stir together cornmeal, flour, sugar, brown sugar, baking soda and salt.

Beat egg slightly and stir in buttermilk and corn oil.

Add liquid to dry ingredients all at once and stir until just moistened.

Fill greased muffin cups ⅔ full and bake for 15-20 minutes until golden brown. Remove from pan immediately.

CRUNCHY CORN OATMEAL MUFFINS

Hearty and wholesome

1 cup flour

1 teaspoon baking powder

¾ teaspoon salt

½ teaspoon baking soda

½ cup yellow cornmeal

½ cup oatmeal

1 cup buttermilk

1 egg, beaten

⅓ cup packed brown sugar

½ cup butter, melted

Makes 18-24 muffins.

Preheat oven to 400 degrees.

Mix flour, baking powder, salt and baking soda. Set aside.

Mix together cornmeal and oatmeal. Add buttermilk. Add egg, sugar and butter to oatmeal mixture. Mix until well blended. Add flour mixture and stir only until just blended. Spoon into greased muffin cups. Bake about 20 minutes or until a rich golden brown.

POPPY SEED MUFFINS

Pecans, raisins and orange peel make these a stand out

¾ cup sugar

¼ cup softened butter

½ teaspoon grated orange peel

2 eggs

2 cups flour

2½ teaspoons baking powder

½ teaspoon salt

¼ teaspoon nutmeg

1 cup milk

½ cup golden raisins

½ cup chopped pecans

5 tablespoons poppy seeds

Makes 18-24 medium muffins.

Preheat oven to 400 degrees.

Cream sugar, butter and orange peel. Add eggs, one at a time, beating well after each addition.

Combine flour, baking powder, salt and nutmeg. Add to creamed mixture, alternately with milk, beating well after each addition.

Fold in raisins, nuts and poppy seeds. Spoon batter into greased muffin cups ¾ full.

Bake about 20 minutes.

OATMEAL APPLE MUFFINS

A serious muffin

1 cup and 2 tablespoons quick-cooking rolled oats

1 cup buttermilk

1 teaspoon vanilla

1 cup sifted flour

½ teaspoon baking soda

1 tablespoon baking powder

1 teaspoon salt

¼ teaspoon cinnamon

½ teaspoon nutmeg

¼ cup coarsely chopped walnuts

1 tart, unpeeled apple, grated

1 large egg

1 cup firmly packed brown sugar

¼ cup melted butter

Makes 18 muffins.

Preheat oven to 400 degrees.

Combine rolled oats, buttermilk and vanilla and set aside.

In another bowl, stir together flour, baking soda, baking powder, salt, cinnamon and nutmeg. Add nuts and apple.

Beat egg, and add brown sugar and melted butter, mixing well. Combine oatmeal mixture and egg mixture and stir well. Add flour mixture and stir just until flour disappears.

Fill greased muffin cups ⅔ full. Sprinkle additional cinnamon on top if desired.

Bake for 15-18 minutes.

Orange Date Muffins

The citrus flavor really comes through

1½ cups sifted flour

1 teaspoon baking powder

1 teaspoon baking soda

½ teaspoon salt

½ cup pitted dates

¼ cup sugar

1 medium unpeeled orange, cut into about 8 pieces

½ cup butter, softened

½ cup sugar

1 large egg, beaten

½ cup fresh orange juice

Makes 18 small muffins.

Preheat oven to 400 degrees.

Mix flour, baking powder, baking soda and salt and set aside.

Process dates with ¼ cup sugar until coarsely chopped (8 pulses). Add orange pieces and pulse until finely chopped. Set aside.

In a large mixing bowl, cream butter and ½ cup sugar together until light and fluffy. Gradually add beaten egg and orange juice and beat well. Add chopped date and orange mixture. Add dry ingredients and mix just until they are incorporated.

Fill greased muffin cups ⅔ full and bake about 15 minutes, until firm to the touch and lightly browned.

ORANGE RAISIN MUFFINS

1 cup sugar

½ cup butter, softened

2 eggs, beaten

1 teaspoon baking soda

1 cup buttermilk

2 cups sifted flour

½ teaspoon salt

1 cup raisins

Peel from 1 orange

Juice from 1 orange

½ cup sugar

Makes 15 medium muffins.

Preheat oven to 400 degrees.

Cream 1 cup sugar and butter until smooth. Add eggs and beat until fluffy.

Add baking soda to buttermilk.

Sift flour and salt together.

Add flour and salt to egg mixture alternately with buttermilk-soda mixture.

Grind raisins and orange peel in food processor and add to batter.

Fill greased muffin cups ⅔ full and bake for about 15 minutes, or until firm to the touch and golden brown.

Mix orange juice and ½ cup sugar. Brush orange juice mixture on muffins while still warm.

DANISH APPLE-COCONUT COFFEE CAKE

Serve warm from the oven for brunch

¾ cup butter

1 cup sugar

3 eggs

1½ cups sifted flour

2 teaspoons baking powder

¼ teaspoon salt

½ cup milk

1¼ cups shredded coconut

2 large tart apples, coarsely grated

¼ cup sliced almonds

2 tablespoons sugar

Serves 12.

Preheat oven to 350 degrees.

Cream butter and sugar until light and fluffy. Add eggs and blend well. Sift flour, baking powder and salt together. Add to egg mixture alternately with the milk. Mix only until smooth. Fold in coconut and apples.

Pour into well-greased 9 by 13-inch pan. Sprinkle almonds and 2 tablespoons of sugar on top. Bake for 25-30 minutes or until top springs back when lightly touched.

Desserts

All luncheons served at Albertina's are planned and tested by a Menu Committee (composed of volunteers) which meets twice each month. The menus emphasize the use of fresh products and regional foods. Eye appeal, nutritional balance and food flavors, as well as public favorites, are prime considerations when planning the three-course luncheons.

FRENCH ALMOND CAKE

Fantastic!

1 cup (8 ounces) almond paste, room temperature

3 eggs

⅔ cup sugar

½ cup butter

¼ cup cake flour

½ teaspoon baking powder

¼ teaspoon salt

Sliced almonds (optional)

Powdered sugar (optional)

Fresh berries or berry sauce (optional)

Whipped cream (optional)

Serves 12.

Preheat oven to 350 degrees.

Grease and flour a 9-inch springform pan.

Beat almond paste until soft and pliable. Add eggs, one at a time. Beat in the sugar. Add butter and beat until the batter is well creamed.

Sift together dry ingredients. Stir into creamed mixture. Pour into the prepared pan. (Sliced almonds may be sprinkled on top.)

Bake for 40-45 minutes. Cool.

Serve sprinkled with powdered sugar and fresh berries on the side, or with berry sauce and whipped cream.

APRICOT-GLAZED ALMOND CAKE

1 cup butter, room temperature

3 cups sugar

1 teaspoon almond extract

1 tablespoon lemon extract

6 eggs

¼ teaspoon baking soda

¼ teaspoon salt

3 cups flour

1 cup sour cream

APRICOT GLAZE

1 cup apricot preserves

2 tablespoons orange juice

1 teaspoon lemon juice

OPTIONAL GLAZE

2 tablespoons orange or lemon juice

¼ cup sugar

Serves 16.

Preheat oven to 325 degrees.

Butter well and flour a Bundt pan.

In a large bowl, beat together sugar, butter, almond and lemon extracts. Add eggs one at a time, beating after each addition.

Sift together flour, soda and salt. Stir into egg mixture alternately with sour cream. Mix until just blended.

Spoon into prepared Bundt pan.

Bake at 325 degrees for 1½ hours or until wooden pick comes out clean. Cool in pan 15 minutes. Turn out.

To prepare Apricot Glaze, thin apricot preserves with orange and lemon juice. Use pastry brush to give cake several coats.

To prepare the Optional Glaze, mix ¼ cup sugar and juice. Drizzle over cake.

VELVET APPLE CAKE

We couldn't decide which sauce is best; you choose

¼ cup vegetable shortening

1 cup sugar

1 egg, well beaten

3 medium apples, unpeeled and diced

1 cup sifted flour

1 teaspoon cinnamon

1 teaspoon baking soda

½ teaspoon salt

½ cup chopped walnuts

BRANDY SAUCE

1 cup half and half

½ cup sugar

½ cup butter

1 tablespoon cornstarch

1 tablespoon cold milk

¼ cup brandy or rum

CARAMEL SAUCE

¼ cup butter

½ cup sugar

½ cup packed brown sugar

½ cup half and half

1 teaspoon vanilla

Serves 8-9.

Preheat oven to 350 degrees.

Cream shortening and sugar. Add beaten egg and mix well. Stir in apples.

Sift flour and add cinnamon, soda, salt and walnuts. Mix well. Gradually add flour mixture to creamed mixture, beating well.

Pour batter into greased and floured 8 by 8-inch cake pan. Bake for 30-35 minutes or until cake tests done.

Serve with either warm Caramel Sauce or Brandy Sauce.

To make Brandy Sauce, combine half and half, sugar and butter in a small pan. Heat ingredients, then simmer for 1 minute. Mix cornstarch with milk. Add to sauce, stirring until sauce has thickened slightly. Add brandy and serve.

For Caramel Sauce, combine all sauce ingredients in a small pan. Cook a few minutes, stirring until slightly thickened. Serve warm.

TUALATIN APPLE CAKE WITH RUM BUTTER SAUCE

Still moist, even when made a day ahead

2 cups flour

2 cups firmly packed light brown sugar

½ cup butter, softened

¾ cup chopped walnuts

1 teaspoon cinnamon

1 teaspoon baking soda

¼ teaspoon salt

1 egg

1 cup sour cream

1 teaspoon vanilla

2 cups unpeeled grated apples

RUM BUTTER SAUCE

2 cups sugar

1 cup butter

1 cup half and half

1 teaspoon vanilla

2 - 3 tablespoons rum

Serves 16.

Preheat oven to 350 degrees.

Butter 2 (9-inch) springform pans.

Combine flour, sugar and butter until mixture is crumbly. Stir in nuts, mixing well. Press 1 cup nut mixture into bottom of each pan.

To remaining nut mixture, add cinnamon, baking soda and salt. Mix well. Beat in egg, sour cream and vanilla. Gently stir in apples and spoon into pans.

Bake until cake pulls away from side, about 25 minutes. Let cool completely before removing from pans. Serve with warm Rum Butter Sauce.

To make Rum Butter Sauce, heat sugar, butter, half and half, vanilla and rum together, making sure sugar is completely dissolved.

APPLE TORTE

Nutty, sweet and easy, too

¾ cup sifted cake flour

1 cup packed light brown sugar

1½ teaspoons baking powder

½ teaspoon salt

Dash mace

Dash cinnamon (or substitute ⅛ teaspoon apple pie spice)

2 eggs, beaten

1½ teaspoons vanilla

1½ cups unpeeled chopped tart apples

¾ cup chopped walnuts

Whipped cream or vanilla ice cream

Serves 8.

Preheat oven to 350 degrees.

Sift together all dry ingredients. Stir in eggs and vanilla. Fold in apples and nuts.

Pour into well-greased 9-inch pie pan.

Bake for 30-35 minutes or until brown and done in the center.

Serve with whipped cream or vanilla ice cream.

CAPITOL CHOCOLATE TORTE

A Gerry Frank favorite

5 eggs

1 cup sugar

1 cup butter

3 ounces semi-sweet chocolate

3 ounces unsweetened chocolate

¼ cup cornstarch, sifted

½ teaspoon vanilla

3 tablespoons orange liqueur

CHOCOLATE GLAZE

6½ ounces semi-sweet chocolate

2 tablespoons unsalted butter

⅓ cup whipping cream

Serves 16.

Preheat oven to 325 degrees.

Grease and flour a 10-inch springform pan.

In the top of a double boiler over hot water, beat eggs and sugar until mixture is very light and almost white in color. Remove from heat. Set aside.

In a saucepan over low heat, melt 1 cup butter and skim off foam. Add 3 ounces of semi-sweet chocolate and the 3 ounces of unsweetened chocolate and stir until melted.

With an electric mixer at low speed, slowly beat the cornstarch into the egg mixture, blending thoroughly.

Stir vanilla and orange liqueur into chocolate. Then whisk into egg mixture. Spoon into prepared pan. Bake for 25-35 minutes or until torte pulls away from sides of pan but a knife inserted in the center DOES NOT come out clean. Cool in pan. Remove rim.

To make glaze, melt 6½ ounces of semi-sweet chocolate and 2 tablespoons butter. Stir in cream blending thoroughly. Spoon over cooled torte. Refrigerate and cool completely.

TOFFEE KAHLUA MADNESS

Yummy!

3 (1⅛ ounce) Heath Bars, finely
   crushed

½ cup walnuts or pecans, finely
   chopped

8 ounces bittersweet chocolate

½ cup butter

½ cup sugar

1½ tablespoons Kahlua

1 teaspoon vanilla

3 eggs at room temperature,
   spearated

¼ teaspoon salt

½ cup flour

3 (1⅛ ounce) Heath Bars,
   coarsely chopped

Serves 8-10.

Preheat oven to 350 degrees

Make crust by combining 3 finely chopped Heath Bars and nuts. Press into the bottom of a 9-inch springform pan. Bake 10 minutes and cool.

Make cake by melting chocolate and butter in the top of a double boiler over medium heat. Add sugar stirring well. Whisk in egg yolks, one at a time. Remove from heat. Stir in Kahlua and vanilla. Set aside. In a separate bowl, beat egg whites and salt until stiff peaks form. Whisk flour into chocolate mixture then fold in egg whites. Pour the batter over the crust and bake for 15 minutes. VERY CAREFULLY, open oven and partially pull out rack. Sprinkle remaining Heath Bars evenly over the top of cake. Bake an additional 10 minutes or until cake tests done. Cool on rack completely. Remove rim.

CHOCOLATE TORTE

A chocolate experience!

½ cup softened butter

¾ cup sugar

1 large egg

1 cup flour

¼ cup unsweetened cocoa

½ teaspoon baking powder

½ teaspoon baking soda

¼ teaspoon salt

¾ cup sour cream

1 ½ teaspoons vanilla

CHOCOLATE GLAZE

3 ounces semi-sweet chocolate

3 tablespoons butter

2 teaspoons light corn syrup

Serves 10.

Preheat oven to 350 degrees.

Cream butter in a large bowl with a mixer set on low speed. Add sugar. Cream well. Add egg and mix well. Sift together all dry ingredients including cocoa. Add dry ingredients gradually, alternating with sour cream. Add vanilla.

Spoon batter into a 9-inch round cake pan which has been greased and lined with parchment. Spread evenly and bake 30-35 minutes or until toothpick comes out clean. Cool 10 minutes and then remove from pan and cool completely.

To prepare Chocolate Glaze, combine ingredients in a heavy quart pan over low heat. Stir frequently until melted and smooth. Remove from heat and stir occasionally until glaze cools and thickens slightly. Place cake on wire rack over waxed paper and spoon glaze on to top and sides of cake. Let cake stand at room temperature until glaze is firm, about 45 minutes.

CHOCOLATE BUNDT CAKE WITH RASPBERRY SAUCE

Chocolate and raspberries—a nice friendship

1 cup margarine

2½ cups sugar

5 eggs

3 cups flour

½ teaspoon salt

½ teaspoon baking powder

½ cup cocoa

1 cup milk

1 teaspoon vanilla

Sweetened whipped cream

RASPBERRY SAUCE

1 (10-ounce) package of frozen
   red raspberries with sugar or
   1¼ cup fresh raspberries
   sweetened with ¼ cup sugar

½ cup currant jelly

2 teaspoons cornstarch

2 teaspoons cold water

Serves 16.

Preheat oven to 325 degrees

Grease well and flour a Bundt pan.

Cream margarine until light and fluffy. Add sugar gradually, creaming well. Beat in eggs one at a time. Sift flour, then measure. Sift again with salt, baking powder and cocoa. Add dry ingredients alternately with milk, beating until just blended. Stir in vanilla. Turn into prepared Bundt pan.

Bake for 1 hour and 20 minutes or until done. Cool 10 minutes on a rack then turn out of pan. Cut when cool. Serve with a dollop of sweetened whipped cream and Raspberry Sauce spooned over all.

To prepare Raspberry Sauce, combine sweetened raspberries with currant jelly in saucepan. Simmer over low heat, stirring frequently, for 10-15 minutes. Let cool. Strain through cheesecloth or double-mesh strainer. Discard seeds and pulp. Put berry juice back into saucepan. Combine cornstarch and cold water to make a smooth paste. Add to juice. Simmer, stirring until clear and slightly thickened. Cool.

Glazed Chocolate Cake

Bring out your best cake plate for this one!

1 ½ cups sugar

½ cup plus 2 tablespoons butter or margarine, softened

2 large eggs

1 ⅔ cups flour

⅔ cup unsweetened cocoa

1 ½ teaspoons baking soda

½ teaspoon salt

½ teaspoon instant espresso coffee powder

1 ½ cups buttermilk

1 teaspoon vanilla

Glaze

4 (1-ounce) squares semi-sweet chocolate

2 tablespoons hot water

2 tablespoons butter

Serves 12-16.

Preheat oven to 350 degrees.

Line bottom of 10-inch springform pan with waxed paper and grease the paper.

In a large bowl, blend sugar and butter or margarine. Beat at high speed for 10 minutes until light and fluffy. Reduce speed. Add eggs and beat well.

Sift together flour, cocoa, baking soda, salt and coffee powder. Add dry ingredients alternately with buttermilk. Add vanilla.

Increase speed to high and beat 2 more minutes. Spoon batter into prepared pan. Bake for 45 minutes or until cake tests done. Cool in pan for 10 minutes. Loosen edges then invert and peel off paper.

When cake is cooled, frost with glaze.

To make glaze, melt chocolate in a double boiler. Add hot water and butter and stir until smooth.

CHOCOLATE SWIRL CAKE

Repeated requests for this recipe convinced us to include it

4 eggs

2 cups sugar

1 cup butter, melted

1½ cups flour

⅓ cup unsweetened cocoa

1 teaspoon vanilla

1 cup coconut

½ cup chopped pecans or walnuts

1 (7-ounce) jar marshmallow creme

FROSTING

¼ cup butter, melted

1½ cups powdered sugar

3 tablespoons unsweetened cocoa

3 tablespoons milk

½ teaspoon vanilla

3 tablespoons coconut

Serves 12.

Preheat oven to 350 degrees.

Beat eggs until light and fluffy. Add sugar gradually and continue beating until batter is very light. Combine butter, flour, cocoa, vanilla, coconut and nuts. Add to egg and sugar mixture. Mix well. Pour into a greased 9 by 13-inch pan. Bake for 30 minutes. Remove from oven. While cake is hot, spread top of cake with marshmallow creme. Make frosting. Spoon frosting on top of marshmallow creme and swirl with back of spoon.

To prepare frosting, place melted butter in a bowl. Combine powdered sugar and cocoa. Add half of the sugar and cocoa mixture to butter, then add half of the milk. Mix to combine, then repeat process. Stir in vanilla and coconut.

Nutcracker Chocolate-Chip Torte

Putting on the "Ritz"

3 eggs

¾ cup sugar

2 cups Ritz cracker crumbs (42 crackers)

¾ cup sugar

1 teaspoon vanilla

1 cup semi-sweet chocolate chips (midgets)

1 cup coarsely chopped walnuts or pecans

Kahlua Cream

1 cup whipping cream

½ teaspoon plain gelatin

1 tablespoon powdered sugar

1 tablespoon Kahlua

Serves 8.

Preheat oven to 350 degrees.

Beat eggs and ¾ cup of sugar until light and fluffy (about 5 minutes). Stir cracker crumbs, second ¾ cup of sugar, vanilla, chocolate chips and nuts into the egg mixture. Blend well.

Pour mixture into a lightly greased 9-inch pie plate. Bake 30 minutes. Cool.

To prepare Kahlua Cream, sprinkle gelatin over unwhipped cream. Let stand 2-3 minutes, then whip until slightly thickened. Add powdered sugar and Kahlua and beat until thick.

Spread over torte or serve individual pieces topped with large dollops of the cream.

FILBERT TORTE WITH MOCHA CREAM

5 eggs, separated

2 cups powdered sugar

1 teaspoon baking powder

2 cups roasted ground filberts
(approximately 1½ cups
whole)

TOPPING

1 cup whipping cream

½ teaspoon gelatin

4 ounces semi-sweet chocolate,
finely chopped

1 tablespoon of strong coffee

Serves 10.

Preheat oven to 325 degrees.

Beat egg whites until stiff peaks form. Set aside.

Beat yolks until light. Gradually add half the powdered sugar, beating well. Sprinkle the baking powder on top. Beat well. Continue adding rest of powdered sugar, beating well. Fold in nuts, then carefully fold in egg whites.

Pour into a 9-inch greased springform pan (bottom only). Bake 1 hour. Cool. Spread with topping.

To prepare topping, sprinkle gelatin over cream and wait 2-3 minutes. Whip until stiff peaks form. Fold in chopped chocolate and coffee. Spread on top of cake.

For a layer cake, split cake through center. Double topping recipe and frost between layers and on top. Refrigerate.

This cake is best made ahead.

NOTE: To roast filberts, place in shallow pan and bake at 275 degrees for 20-30 minutes until the skins crack. Bundle nuts into a dish towel and rub nuts together until a majority of the papery skins have fallen off.

MARVELOUS OATMEAL CAKE

1 cup quick oatmeal

1½ cups boiling water

½ cup butter

1 cup packed brown sugar

1½ cups sugar

2 eggs, beaten

1 cup sifted flour

1 teaspoon baking soda

1 teaspoon cinnamon

½ teaspoon nutmeg

½ teaspoon cloves

1 teaspoon vanilla

½ cup chopped nuts

Whipped cream (optional)

Serves 12.

Preheat oven to 350 degrees.

Combine oatmeal and boiling water. Let stand 15-20 minutes.

Cream butter and sugars until light and creamy. Add eggs and continue beating. Stir in cooled oatmeal mixture. Sift together flour, baking soda and spices. Gradually add dry ingredients to batter. Mix well. Add vanilla. Fold in walnuts.

Pour into a greased and floured 9 by 13 by 2-inch baking pan. Bake 45-55 minutes or until cake tests done. Cake may be served with a dollop of sweetened whipped cream.

Fresh Pear Bundt Cake

2 cups sugar

1 cup vegetable oil

4 large eggs

2 cups flour

2 teaspoons baking powder

2 teaspoons baking soda

1 teaspoon salt

½ teaspoon nutmeg

1 teaspoon cinnamon

3 very firm pears, unpeeled and grated

¾ cup chopped walnuts

1 teaspoon vanilla

Serves 16.

Preheat oven to 325 degrees.

Combine oil and sugar, beating well. Add eggs one at a time, beating after each addition.

Sift together dry ingredients. Add to first mixture, blending thoroughly. Fold in pears, walnuts and vanilla.

Spoon into a greased and floured Bundt pan, spreading evenly.

Bake until cake tests done, about 55-65 minutes.

AUTUMN PLUM CAKE

Little Jack Horner never had it so good

1 cup sugar

½ cup packed brown sugar

¾ cup oil

1 egg, beaten

1 tablespoon freshly grated
   orange peel

2 cups flour

¼ teaspoon salt

1 teaspoon baking soda

1 cup buttermilk

2 cups purple plums (Italian
   prunes), pitted and cut into
   eighths

TOPPING

½ cup granulated sugar

1½ teaspoons cinnamon

½ cup chopped walnuts or
   pecans

Whipped cream (optional)

Serves 12.

Preheat oven to 350 degrees.

In large mixing bowl, beat together sugars, oil, beaten egg and orange peel. Sift, then measure flour. Add salt and baking soda to flour, mixing well. Add flour mixture gradually to sugar mixture, alternating with buttermilk. Stir in plums. Pour into greased 9 by 13-inch pan.

Combine topping ingredients. Mix well and sprinkle evenly over batter. Bake for 45 minutes or until done. Serve with whipped cream if desired.

Poppy Seed Cake with Lemon Curd

3 eggs

2 cups sugar

1 cup vegetable oil

3 cups sifted flour

1½ teaspoons baking soda

½ teaspoon salt

1½ cups canned evaporated milk

⅓ cup poppy seeds

Lemon Curd

4 eggs

2 cups sugar

⅛ teaspoon salt

½ cup fresh lemon juice

¼ cup butter

2 tablespoons grated lemon rind

Serves 16.

Preheat oven to 325 degrees.

Grease and flour a Bundt pan.

Beat eggs. Add sugar gradually, then oil, beating until fluffy. Sift dry ingredients together. Add to egg mixture alternately with milk. Mix well. Add poppy seeds and mix again.

Pour into prepared Bundt pan and bake for 55-65 minutes or until knife comes out clean. Serve with Lemon Curd.

To prepare Lemon Curd, beat eggs, sugar and salt. Stir in lemon juice, butter and lemon rind. Cook in top of double boiler, stirring occasionally, until thick and smooth. Cool to room temperature. Store in refrigerator.

PUMPKIN CAKE WITH RICH RUM SAUCE

1 cup butter

2 cups sugar

4 eggs

1½ cups pumpkin

1 tablespoon dark rum

3½ cups sifted flour

1 tablespoon baking powder

2 teaspoons pumpkin pie spice

½ teaspoon salt

RICH RUM SAUCE

2 cups orange juice

¾ cup sugar

½ teaspoon pumpkin pie spice

3 tablespoons cornstarch

¼ cup dark rum

2 tablespoons butter

Serves 16.

Preheat oven to 325 degrees.

Grease well and flour a Bundt pan.

Cream butter and sugar until light and fluffy. Add eggs, one at a time, beating well after each addition. Combine pumpkin and rum and add to cake batter. Sift together flour, baking powder, pumpkin pie spice and salt. Add gradually to cake batter, mixing well.

Spoon into prepared Bundt pan and bake for 1¼ hours or until cake tests done.

Serve with Rich Rum Sauce.

To prepare Rich Rum Sauce, combine orange juice, sugar and spice in saucepan and bring to a boil. Mix cornstarch and rum and stir into orange juice mixture. Cook until sauce is clear and slightly thickened. Stir in butter.

Rhubarb Cake

½ cup margarine

1½ cups sugar

1 egg

2 cups flour

1 teaspoon baking soda

½ teaspoon salt

1 cup buttermilk

1 teaspoon vanilla

2 cups chopped rhubarb

Topping

½ cup brown sugar

1 teaspoon cinnamon

¼ cup margarine

Whipped cream or ice cream

Serves 12.

Preheat oven to 350 degrees.

Cream margarine and sugar. Add egg and beat well. Sift dry ingredients together. Add dry ingredients to creamed mixture, alternating with buttermilk. Add vanilla. Add rhubarb and mix thoroughly. Spread into greased 9 by 13-inch pan. Make topping and distribute over top of cake.

Bake for 35-45 minutes or until done. Serve with sweetened whipped cream or ice cream.

To prepare topping, combine brown sugar and cinnamon. Cut in margarine.

Rhubarb Streusel Cake

Remember this recipe for rhubarb season

1½ cups packed brown sugar

½ cup butter, softened

1 egg

2 cups sifted flour

1 teaspoon baking soda

½ teaspoon salt

1 cup sour cream

1 teaspoon vanilla

1½ cups rhubarb, cut in ½-inch pieces

Whipping cream (optional)

Topping

½ cup sugar

½ cup chopped walnuts

1 tablespoon melted butter

1 teaspoon cinnamon

Serves 12.

Preheat oven to 350 degrees.

Mix topping ingredients together until crumbly. Set aside.

Cream together brown sugar, butter and egg. Sift together flour, soda and salt. Add dry ingredients alternately with sour cream and vanilla to the creamed mixture.

Fold in rhubarb. Spoon into buttered 9 by 13-inch pan. Sprinkle with the reserved topping.

Bake 45-50 minutes or until set in the center.

Serve slightly warm with whipped cream.

DERBY PIE

A chocolate-chip cookie in a pie crust!

2 eggs

1 cup sugar

½ cup margarine, melted

½ cup flour

1 teaspoon vanilla

1 cup chocolate chips

1 cup walnuts or pecans

1 (9-inch) unbaked pie crust

Sweetened whipped cream or
   ice cream

Serves 8-10.

Preheat oven to 350 degrees.

Beat eggs until very fluffy. Gradually add sugar, beating well. Add melted and cooled margarine, flour and vanilla. Mix well. Fold in chocolate chips and walnuts or pecans.

Spoon into unbaked pie crust. Bake for 30-40 minutes or until center is firm. Cool. Serve with sweetened whipped cream or ice cream.

DATE MERINGUE

An oldie but goodie!

3 egg whites

1 cup sugar

2 teaspoons baking powder

1 teaspoon vanilla

¾ cup chopped walnuts

1 cup chopped dates

12 soda crackers, finely crushed

1 cup whipping cream, whipped
   and sweetened

Serves 8-10.

Preheat oven to 350 degrees.

Beat egg whites until stiff, slowly adding sugar. Add baking powder and vanilla. Fold in nuts, dates and cracker crumbs. Bake in greased, 9-inch square pan for 30-35 minutes.

Cut in squares and serve with whipped cream.

BAVARIAN APPLE TORTE

In all the best cookbooks

½ cup butter

⅓ cup sugar

¼ teaspoon vanilla

1 cup flour

1 (8-ounce) package cream
    cheese, softened

¼ cup sugar

1 egg

½ teaspoon vanilla

⅓ cup sugar

½ teaspoon cinnamon

4 cups sliced peeled apples

¼ cup sliced almonds

Serves 8-10.

Preheat oven to 425 degrees.

Cream butter, ⅓ cup sugar and ¼ teaspoon vanilla. Blend in flour. Spread dough onto the bottom and 1½ inches up the sides of a 9-inch springform pan. (Chill for a few minutes if the dough is too soft.)

Combine cream cheese and ¼ cup sugar. Mix well. Add egg and ½ teaspoon vanilla and mix. Pour into pastry-lined pan.

Combine ⅓ cup sugar and cinnamon. Toss apples in this mixture. Arrange apples over cream cheese layer and sprinkle with nuts.

Bake at 425 degrees for 10 minutes. Reduce heat to 350 degrees and continue baking for about 25 minutes or until apples are tender. Loosen torte from rim of pan. Cool before removing the rim.

BLUEBERRY TART

Beautiful and soooooo good! The best blueberry dessert we have found.

CRUST

1 cup flour

⅛ teaspoon salt

2 tablespoons sugar

½ cup cold butter

1 tablespoon white vinegar

FILLING

5 cups blueberries, divided

⅔ cup sugar

⅛ teaspoon cinnamon

3 tablespoons flour

½ cup whipping cream,
    whipped and sweetened

Serves 8.

Preheat oven to 400 degrees.

To make crust, place flour, salt and sugar in a food processor. Pulse to mix. Cut butter in chunks and add to flour mixture. Pulse several times until the dough resembles coarse crumbs. Sprinkle vinegar over the top and pulse just a few times until ball starts to form. Remove from processor and press into a ball.

With lightly floured fingers, press into a greased, 9-inch springform pan, about ¼ inch thick and extending up the side 1¼ inches.

To make filling, put 3 cups blueberries into the crust. Mix sugar, cinnamon and flour. Sprinkle evenly over berries. Bake on lowest rack in 400-degree oven for 25 minutes. Remove from oven and gently stir sugar mixture into berries. Reduce heat to 350 degrees and bake 15-20 minutes until crust is brown and filling bubbles.

Remove and sprinkle with the remaining 2 cups of berries. Cool and serve with whipped cream.

DEEP-DISH APPLE PIE

The rum makes the difference

Dough for single pie crust (use your favorite recipe)

8 large tart apples, Newton or Granny Smith

1 cup sugar

1/8 teaspoon salt

Juice and grated rind of 1 orange

1/4 cup butter

1/4 cup rum

1 cup whipping cream, whipped and sweetened

Serves 8-10.

Preheat oven to 400 degrees.

Peel, core and slice apples, putting them into a 9 by 13-inch baking dish. Sprinkle apples with sugar, salt, rind and juice. Dot with small pieces of butter.

Roll out dough to fit top of baking dish and cut out small hole in center. Place dough over apples and press firmly against rim of baking dish. Trim off any excess crust.

Bake pie at 450 degrees for 15 minutes. Reduce temperature to 350 degrees. Bake about 45 minutes longer, or until crust is golden and apples tender. Remove pie from oven and pour rum through a small funnel into the hole in the crust.

Serve pie warm, topped with whipped cream.

MARIONBERRY COBBLER

A real Oregon dessert for your out-of-town guests

2½ cups marionberries or
    blackberries

¾ cup water

1 cup sifted flour

2 teaspoons baking powder

⅛ teaspoon salt

¼ cup butter

1 cup sugar, divided

½ cup milk

1 cup berry juice

Nutmeg

Serves 6.

Preheat oven to 375 degrees.

In a saucepan bring berries and water just to simmer. Strain berries and save juice for topping.

Sift flour, baking powder and salt together. Set aside. Cream butter until soft and smooth. Gradually add ½ cup sugar, creaming until light and fluffy. Add sifted dry ingredients alternately with milk, beating until smooth after each addition.

Pour batter into greased, 8-inch square pan. Spoon drained berries over batter and sprinkle with remaining ½ cup sugar. Pour 1 cup of reserved berry juice over all. Sprinkle with nutmeg.

Bake 45-50 minutes or until done. As the cobbler bakes, the crust will rise to the top. Serve warm with cream or ice cream.

NOTE: Frozen berries may be used. Thaw well and use thawed juice for part of the water when cooking berries.

PEACH KUCHEN

Fresh peaches? This recipe is exceptional!

CRUST

1 ¼ cups flour

¼ teaspoon salt

½ cup cold unsalted butter, cut into 6 pieces

2 tablespoons sour cream

FILLING

3 large egg yolks

⅓ cup sour cream

1 cup sugar

¼ cup flour

¼ teaspoon salt

1 pound (4 medium sized) fresh, ripe peaches, peeled and thickly sliced

Serves 8.

Preheat oven to 375 degrees.

In food processor, using metal blade, process flour, salt and butter until crumbly. Add sour cream and let machine run until dough just forms a ball (4-6 seconds).

As an alternate method, cut butter into flour and salt with pastry blender. Add sour cream and mix lightly.

Press dough into a 9-inch tart or pie pan to cover sides and bottom evenly. Bake 20 minutes or until lightly browned. Cool.

Reduce heat to 350 degrees to bake filling.

To make filling, beat egg yolks. Add sour cream and blend.

Mix sugar, flour and salt. Add to egg mixture. Beat well.

Pour half the custard mixture into prepared crust. Arrange peach slices on top of custard. Pour remaining custard over peaches.

Bake at 350 degrees for 40-50 minutes or until custard is set and top is lightly browned. Serve warm or at room temperature.

PECAN TORTE

4 large egg whites

1 ⅓ cups finely ground graham
    cracker crumbs

1 cup sugar

1 ⅓ teaspoons baking powder

1 ½ teaspoons vanilla

1 cup coarsely chopped pecans

Whipped cream (topping)

Serves 8.

Preheat oven to 350 degrees.

Beat egg whites until they just hold stiff peaks. Fold in graham cracker crumbs, sugar, baking powder and vanilla. Add pecans last.

Pour into greased, 9-inch pie pan. Bake for 25-30 minutes or until golden and puffed. Let cool and serve with whipped cream or ice cream.

SWEDISH CREAM

Light and luscious

1 ¾ teaspoons gelatin

2 tablespoons cold water

1 ½ cups whipping cream,
    unwhipped

⅓ cup sugar

½ cup sour cream

½ cup plain yogurt

¾ teaspoon vanilla

2 tablespoons Grand Marnier or
    curaçao (orange liqueur)

Serves 6.

Sprinkle gelatin over water in a small bowl. Stir and let sit three minutes.

Combine whipping cream, sugar and softened gelatin in a saucepan. Place over medium heat to dissolve gelatin. Do not allow to boil. Cool in refrigerator, stirring frequently until mixture is room temperature. Fold in sour cream, yogurt, vanilla and liqueur. Stir until smooth. Pour into stemmed glasses or molds. Refrigerate several hours or overnight. Serve topped with fresh berries or berry sauce.

Purple Plum Kuchen

Butter Pastry

1½ cups flour

¼ cup sugar

¼ teaspoon salt

½ cup butter

1 egg yolk, beaten

1 tablespoon cold water

Fruit Layer

3 cups pitted, sliced Italian plums

½ cup sugar

1½ teaspoons cinnamon

Cheesecake Layer

8 ounces cream cheese, room temperature

3 eggs

¾ cup sour cream

1 teaspoon vanilla

½ teaspoon grated lemon peel

¾ cup sugar

Powdered sugar

Serves 9.

Preheat oven to 350 degrees.

To make pastry, combine flour, sugar and salt. Cut in butter until mixture is mealy. Stir in egg yolk and water. Work into a ball. Press evenly into a 9-inch square pan. Bake 10 minutes.

To make fruit layer, arrange fruit on top of baked pastry. Sprinkle evenly with ½ cup sugar and cinnamon. Bake 15 minutes.

To make cheesecake layer, beat cheese until soft and fluffy. Continue beating, adding eggs one at a time. Beat in remaining ingredients and pour over fruit. Bake 35 minutes longer, or until center of kuchen is set and top is lightly browned. Sift powdered sugar over top just before serving.

STRAWBERRY SHORTCAKE

Absolutely the best shortcake recipe! Try it with other berries.

2 cups sifted flour

4 teaspoons baking powder

¾ teaspoon salt

⅓ cup sugar

½ cup shortening

⅔ cup milk

3 cups sliced strawberries

¼ cup sugar

2 cups whipping cream

2 tablespoons powdered sugar

Serves 8-10.

Preheat oven to 375 degrees.

To make shortcake, combine flour, baking powder, salt and ⅓ cup sugar. Mix well. Cut shortening into flour mixture with pastry blender or food processor. Add milk and stir by hand until just barely mixed. Drop by large spoonfuls onto greased baking sheet. (Makes 8-10 biscuits.) Bake for 12-15 minutes or until golden brown and done in the center. Cool.

To put shortcakes together, cut the top ⅓ off each and set aside for lids. Combine sliced strawberries and sugar about 10 minutes before using. Whip cream until stiff and add powdered sugar.

Place each shortcake bottom on plate. Spoon on about ⅓ cup whipped cream. Add about ⅓ cup sweetened strawberries, then a spoonful of whipped cream, put on the lid and enjoy!

BLUEBERRY CREAM CHEESE TART

1 (9-inch) baked pie shell

BLUEBERRY TOPPING

¼ cup cornstarch

¾ cup sugar

⅛ teaspoon salt

¼ cup cold water

3 cups blueberries

1 tablespoon lemon juice

1 tablespoon butter

FILLING

4 ounces cream cheese, softened

¾ cup whipping cream, unwhipped

3 tablespoons powdered sugar

¼ teaspoon vanilla

½ teaspoon grated lemon peel

1 teaspoon fresh lemon juice

Serves 8.

To make Blueberry Topping, combine cornstarch, sugar and salt in a saucepan. Add water and mix well. Add blueberries and cook over medium heat, stirring constantly until the mixture comes to a boil, thickens and has a shiny look. Add lemon juice and butter and stir. Cool.

To make filling, beat softened cream cheese in electric mixer until smooth and creamy. Gradually add whipping cream, alternating with powdered sugar. Add vanilla, lemon peel and juice.

To assemble pie, spoon filling into baked pie shell. Smooth surface. Add cooled blueberry topping. Chill and serve. May add a spoonful of sweetened whipped cream to each serving.

CHEESE BLINTZES WITH FRESH STRAWBERRIES

DESSERT CREPES

1 cup flour

1½ cups milk

2 eggs

2 tablespoons sugar

1 tablespoon vegetable oil

⅛ teaspoon salt

FILLING

1 cup ricotta cheese

⅔ cup cottage cheese, blended in food processor

¼ cup powdered sugar

½ teaspoon grated lemon peel

½ teaspoon vanilla

1 teaspoon orange-flavored liqueur

TOPPING

3 cups sliced fresh strawberries

2 tablespoons sugar

½ cup whipping cream

1 tablespoon powdered sugar

¼ teaspoon vanilla

Serves 8 (16 crepes).

To prepare dessert crepes, combine all ingredients in a bowl and beat until blended. You may also use a blender.

Lightly grease a 6-inch skillet and place over medium heat. When hot, remove from heat and spoon in 2 tablespoons of batter. Lift and tilt skillet to spread batter evenly. Return to heat and brown on one side only. Remove by inverting skillet on paper toweling.

Combine all filling ingredients. Mix well. Spoon 2 tablespoons of filling into each crepe. Fold or roll crepes and place in a large, lightly greased baking dish. Set aside.

Preheat oven to 200 degrees.

Fifteen minutes before serving time, add sugar to sliced strawberries. Whip cream, and add powdered sugar and vanilla.

Warm blintzes in oven 4-5 minutes.

Serve two warmed blintzes on a plate topped with strawberries and a dollop of sweetened whipped cream.

NOTE: Crepes may be made ahead and frozen. Stack crepes between two layers of waxed paper and seal in a freezer bag and freeze.

CHOCOLATE MOCHA ANGEL PIE

Heavenly!

MERINGUE CRUST

2 large egg whites, room temperature

⅛ teaspoon cream of tartar

½ cup superfine sugar

½ cup finely chopped walnuts or pecans

FILLING

4½ ounces semi-sweet chocolate bits

3 tablespoons strong coffee

1 teaspoon vanilla

1 cup whipping cream, whipped

Serves 8.

Preheat oven to 275 degrees.

To make meringue crust, beat egg whites until frothy. Add cream of tartar and beat until stiff. Slowly add sugar, 1-2 tablespoons at a time, beating until glossy. Fold in chopped nuts. Pour into well-greased, 9-inch pie pan.

Bake 45-60 minutes. Turn off oven and leave crust in two hours or overnight.

To make filling, melt chocolate bits and coffee in top of double boiler. Stir until smooth. Add vanilla. Cool. Fold in whipped cream.

Pour into Meringue Crust. Chill several hours. May be garnished with chocolate curls.

LEMON ANGEL PIE

MERINGUE SHELL

4 egg whites, room temperature

¼ teaspoon cream of tartar

1 cup superfine sugar

1 teaspoon vinegar

½ teaspoon vanilla

FILLING

4 egg yolks

½ cup sugar

3 tablespoons fresh lemon juice

2 teaspoons grated lemon rind

3 tablespoons hot water

1 cup whipping cream

1 teaspoon vanilla

Serves 8-10.

Preheat oven to 275 degrees.

To prepare meringue shell, beat egg whites until soft peaks form. Add cream of tartar. Beat in sugar gradually until stiff peaks form. Blend in vanilla and vinegar. Bake in greased, 9-inch springform pan for 45 minutes. Cool.

To prepare filling, combine egg yolks, sugar, lemon juice, lemon rind and water in the top of a double boiler. Cook until just thickened, stirring constantly. Remove from heat. Cool to room temperature.

Beat whipping cream with vanilla until stiff. Spread half the whipped cream over baked and cooled meringue. Spread lemon filling over whipped cream. Top with remaining whipped cream. Chill overnight.

As an alternate method, fold whipped cream into cooled lemon filling. Spread over meringue and chill.

LEMON SILK TORTE

Stunning presentation and fabulous taste

CRUST

6 large egg whites, room
    temperature

1 cup sugar

1½ teaspoons lemon juice

¼ teaspoon almond extract

1½ teaspoons vanilla

4½ tablespoons flour

¾ teaspoon baking powder

1 cup finely ground almonds,
    natural or blanched, unsalted

FILLING

1½ teaspoons unflavored
    gelatin

3 tablespoons cold water

6 egg yolks

¾ cup sugar

9 tablespoons fresh lemon juice

1½ teaspoons grated lemon rind

1½ cups whipping cream

STRAWBERRY SAUCE

1 small box frozen strawberries
    with sugar (garnish)

Serves 10-12.

Preheat oven to 325 degrees.

Grease and flour a 10-inch springform pan. Beat egg whites until foamy. Beat in sugar gradually until soft peaks form. Add lemon juice, almond extract and vanilla. Beat until stiff peaks form.

Combine flour, baking powder and ground almonds. Gently fold mixture into egg whites. Spoon into prepared springform pan, level, and bake for 40 minutes or until crust pulls away from side of pan. Cool completely on rack.

To prepare filling, sprinkle gelatin over cold water in a small bowl. Let stand 15 minutes.

In the top of a double boiler, beat egg yolks and sugar. Stir in lemon juice and lemon rind. Cook, stirring over simmering water for 10-12 minutes or until mixture thickens. Remove top of double boiler from water and whisk in gelatin. Return top of double boiler to water and whisk until custard is thick (approximately 7 minutes). Do not allow to boil. Remove pan from water. Cool, stirring frequently.

Beat the whipping cream until stiff. Fold into the cooled lemon filling. Pour into cooled meringue crust and chill overnight.

To make sauce, blend sugared strawberries until smooth. Thin with water if necessary.

To serve, cut into 10-12 pieces, place on plates and drizzle strawberry sauce onto plates. May garnish the top with a dollop of sweetened whipped cream and a fanned strawberry.

STRAWBERRY CLOUD

A special dessert traditionally served on Albertina's anniversary

MERINGUES

4 egg whites

⅛ teaspoon salt

¼ teaspoon cream of tartar

1 cup sugar

1 teaspoon vanilla

FILLINGS

6 ounces chocolate chips

3 tablespoons water

3 cups whipping cream

⅓ cup sugar

2 cups sliced fresh strawberries

2 cups fresh whole or halved
  berries

Serves 10-12.

Preheat oven to 300 degrees.

Line baking sheets with parchment paper and trace 3 circles, each 9 inches in diameter.

To make meringues, beat egg whites until soft peaks form. Mix salt and cream of tartar with sugar. Gradually add sugar mixture to egg whites, beating constantly. Continue to beat until meringue makes stiff, glossy peaks. Add vanilla.

Spread meringue evenly on each circle. Bake 45-50 minutes. Turn off oven and leave meringues in two hours or overnight. Remove from oven and carefully take off paper, using a metal spatula.

To prepare fillings, combine chocolate chips and water in a saucepan. Heat and stir until melted. Whip cream until stiff and add sugar.

To assemble, place a meringue on a serving plate. Spread meringue with ⅓ of the chocolate. Cover the chocolate with ⅓ of the whipped cream, then ½ of the sliced berries. Add a second meringue to top and repeat chocolate, whipped cream and sliced strawberry layers. Add third meringue to top. Spread chocolate and whipped cream layers as above. Arrange whole or halved berries on top. Refrigerate for two hours. To serve, cut in wedges.

As an alternative, make individual meringue shells, 15 (3-inch) meringues. Bake for 30-35 minutes, then leave in turned-off oven overnight. Spread with layer of chocolate sauce, then top with whipped cream and strawberries.

STRAWBERRY TORTE

Check out this meringue crust. You'll love it!

MERINGUE CRUST

3 egg whites

½ teaspoon baking powder

1 cup sugar

½ teaspoon almond flavoring

½ teaspoon vanilla

⅔ cup finely crushed soda crackers

½ cup chopped walnuts

TOPPING

1 cup whipping cream

¼ teaspoon gelatin

1½ teaspoons powdered sugar

½ teaspoon vanilla

2 cups sliced strawberries

Serves 8.

Preheat oven to 300 degrees.

Beat egg whites until frothy. Add baking powder and continue beating until soft peaks form. Add sugar gradually, beating until stiff peaks form. Add almond flavoring and vanilla. Add crushed soda crackers and nuts and mix gently.

Pour into greased, 9-inch pie pan.

Bake 40-50 minutes. Cool.

To make topping, sprinkle gelatin over cream. Let stand 2 minutes.

Whip cream with powdered sugar and vanilla. Spread into cooled meringue crust. Refrigerate at least two hours.

Add sliced berries on top of torte just before serving.

CHOCOLATE PECAN MERINGUE TORTE

This is to die for!

MERINGUE

4 egg whites, room temperature

½ teaspoon cream of tartar

1 cup sugar

1 cup chopped pecans

FILLING

2 cups whipping cream

¾ cup chocolate sauce
   (homemade or purchased)

1 teaspoon vanilla

2 (1.4-ounce size) Heath Bars

Serves 10-12.

Preheat oven to 275 degrees.

Beat egg whites until foamy. Add cream of tartar and beat until soft peaks form. Slowly add sugar, 1 tablespoon at a time, until mixture is stiff. Fold in pecans.

Cover cookie sheet with parchment paper. Draw 2 (8-inch) circles on paper. Divide meringue between circles and spread evenly, forming meringue rounds. Bake for 1 hour. Turn off oven and leave in unopened oven for several hours. Remove from oven and gently peel off paper. Set aside. May be wrapped in air-tight container for several days at this point.

To prepare filling, whip cream until very stiff. Fold in chocolate sauce and vanilla. Spread ½ of filling over 1 meringue layer. Top with second meringue layer and spread top with remaining filling. Crumble 2 Heath Bars for garnish and sprinkle on top. Freeze. To serve, cut when frozen or just slightly thawed.

GRAND MARNIER FROZEN PIE

Fast and fabulous

1 baked 9-inch graham cracker
   crust

1½ pints vanilla ice cream

5 macaroons

4 teaspoons Grand Marnier

½ cup whipping cream

2 tablespoons sliced toasted
   almonds

2 teaspoons confectioners' sugar

Serves 8.

Soften ice cream. Crumble macaroons. Whip cream. Toast almonds. Mix ice cream, macaroons and Grand Marnier. Fold in whipped cream. Spoon into prepared graham cracker crust. Sprinkle surface lightly with almonds and sugar. Cover with plastic wrap and freeze.

COFFEE TORTONI

A perfect light finish

2 egg whites

2 tablespoons instant coffee
   powder

¼ teaspoon salt

¼ cup sugar

2 cups whipping cream

½ cup sugar

¼ teaspoon almond extract

2 teaspoons vanilla

¾ cup finely chopped toasted
   almonds, divided

Serves 10-12.

Beat egg whites until frothy. Add coffee powder and salt. Gradually add ¼ cup sugar, beating until stiff peaks form.

Whip cream, gradually adding ½ cup sugar, almond extract and vanilla. Fold cream mixture and ½ cup toasted almonds into the egg whites.

Spoon mixture into individual molds or into paper-lined muffin tins. Cover and freeze.

To serve, unmold or remove paper linings. Serve in sherbet glasses. Sprinkle remaining ¼ cup of almonds on top.

FESTIVAL CRANBERRY TORTE

Stunning presentation—wonderful holiday dessert

CRUST

1 cup graham cracker crumbs

⅓ cup chopped walnuts

3 tablespoons sugar

¼ cup melted butter

FILLING

1½ cups fresh finely ground or
   chopped cranberries

1 cup sugar

2 egg whites, unbeaten

1 tablespoon orange juice

1 teaspoon vanilla

½ teaspoon salt

1 cup whipping cream

Additional whipping cream
   (garnish)

Serves 8-10.

Combine crust ingredients and blend well. Press into bottom of a 9-inch springform pan. Chill.

In large bowl of electric mixer, combine cranberries and sugar. Let stand 5 minutes. Add egg whites, orange juice, vanilla and salt. Beat on slow speed until frothy, then at high speed 6-8 minutes or until stiff peaks form.

In another bowl, beat whipping cream until soft peaks form. Fold whipped cream into cranberry mixture. Spoon into crust and cover. Freeze until firm. Serve with sweetened whipped cream.

GRASSHOPPER PIE

A colorful choice for Christmas or St. Patrick's Day

CRUST

1¼ cups finely crushed chocolate wafer crumbs, reserving 3 tablespoons for garnish

¼ cup butter, melted

FILLING

1 quart vanilla ice cream

2 tablespoons green creme de menthe

1 tablespoon white creme de cocoa

A few drops of green food coloring

A few drops of peppermint flavoring

Serves 8.

Preheat oven to 350 degrees.

To make crust, blend chocolate wafer crumbs and melted butter thoroughly. Press gently onto bottom and sides of a greased, 9-inch pie pan. Bake for 8 minutes. Cool.

To prepare filling, soften ice cream. Stir in creme de menthe and creme de cocoa. Add a few drops of green food coloring. Mix well. Add peppermint flavoring to enhance the mint taste. (Avoid the temptation to add more creme de menthe or creme de cocoa. Pie will not freeze.) Pour into crumb crust, cover and freeze overnight. Garnish with reserved chocolate crumbs.

LEMON DREAM PIE

Luscious and lemony

CRUST

1 cup vanilla wafer crumbs

2 tablespoons melted butter

FILLING

3 egg yolks, beaten

½ cup sugar

2 tablespoons cold water

¼ cup fresh lemon juice

Grated rind of 2 lemons

3 egg whites

½ cup sugar

1 cup whipping cream

Sweetened whipped cream

Serves 8.

Combine crumbs and melted butter. Reserve 2-3 tablespoons to sprinkle on top of pie. Press rest of crumbs into bottom and sides of 9-inch pie tin. It will be thinly covered. Do not bake. Set aside.

Combine beaten egg yolks, ½ cup sugar, water, lemon juice and rind. Mix well. Place in top of double boiler. Cook over hot water, stirring frequently until thick. Remove from heat and cool.

When yolk mixture is cool, beat egg whites until soft peaks form. Gradually add ½ cup sugar and beat until stiff. Fold into egg yolk mixture. Whip cream and fold into egg-lemon mixture. Pour filling into crumb crust. Sprinkle top with reserved crumbs. Cover and freeze. Serve with a dollop of sweetened whipped cream.

FROZEN LEMON MOUSSE

Light and lemony—one of the best of Albertina's

CRUMB CRUST

¼ cup butter, softened

2 tablespoons light brown sugar

½ cup flour

¼ cup chopped walnuts

FILLING

4 egg yolks, beaten

½ cup fresh lemon juice

1½ tablespoons grated lemon rind

¼ cup sugar

4 egg whites

⅛ teaspoon cream of tartar

⅛ teaspoon salt

¾ cup sugar

1½ cups whipping cream, whipped until stiff

Sweetened whipped cream and mint leaf (garnish)

Serves 10.

Preheat oven to 400 degrees.

Mix together crust ingredients and put in a flat pan. Bake, stirring often until crumbs are brown. Cool.

Press crumbs firmly into the bottom of an ungreased, 9-inch springform pan, reserving 2 tablespoons to sprinkle on top.

To prepare filling, combine egg yolks, lemon juice, rind and ¼ cup sugar. Blend thoroughly.

Beat egg whites until foamy. Add cream of tartar and salt. Beat until soft peaks form. Slowly add ¾ cup sugar, 2 tablespoons at a time, and beat until whites are stiff and shiny. Fold the egg-yolk mixture and the whipped cream carefully into the egg whites. Spoon into springform pan. Sprinkle with remaining crumbs. Cover and freeze.

Serve frozen with a dollop of whipped cream and a fresh mint leaf on each serving.

MOCHA FUDGE PIE

Tempt your guests with this mocha version of mud pie

CRUST

1 ¼ cups finely crushed
    chocolate wafer crumbs

3 tablespoons melted butter

FUDGE SAUCE

3 squares unsweetened
    chocolate

¼ cup butter

⅔ cup sugar

⅛ teaspoon salt

⅔ cup evaporated milk

1 teaspoon vanilla

FILLING

3 cups softened coffee ice
    cream

Serves 8.

Preheat oven to 350 degrees.

To make crust, combine chocolate crumbs and butter. Lightly press onto bottom and sides of greased, 9-inch pie pan. Bake for 8 minutes. Cool.

To prepare Fudge Sauce, melt chocolate and butter in top of double boiler. Remove from heat and add remaining ingredients. Return to heat, simmer and stir about 4 minutes or until thick. Cool. Sauce may be made ahead and refrigerated until needed.

To assemble pie, fill baked and cooled crust with ice cream. Smooth top. Top with room temperature Fudge Sauce, using as much as desired. Cover and freeze.

FROZEN PUMPKIN PIE

The gingersnap crust compliments this great-tasting pumpkin pie

GINGERSNAP CRUST

½ cup finely chopped walnuts

1 cup crushed gingersnap
    crumbs

3 tablespoons sugar

3 tablespoons melted butter

FILLING

1 pint vanilla ice cream,
    softened

1 cup pumpkin

¾ cup sugar

¼ teaspoon salt

½ teaspoon ginger

¼ teaspoon nutmeg

1 cup whipping cream

BUTTERSCOTCH SAUCE

1½ cups brown sugar

½ cup white corn syrup

¼ cup butter

1 teaspoon vanilla

½ cup cream

Serves 8.

Preheat oven to 350 degrees.

To make crust, combine walnuts, gingersnaps and sugar. Add melted butter and mix until moistened. Press into a 9-inch pie pan. Bake 7-8 minutes. Cool.

To make filling, spread softened ice cream on bottom of cooled crust. Place in the freezer while preparing pumpkin layer.

Mix pumpkin, sugar, salt and spices. Whip cream until stiff. Fold whipped cream into pumpkin mixture. Pour pumpkin cream mixture over ice cream layer and spread evenly. Freeze overnight. Serve with Butterscotch Sauce, if desired.

To make sauce, mix all ingredients in a saucepan except vanilla and cream. Heat over medium heat, stirring until mixture comes to a boil. Remove from heat and stir in cream and vanilla. Cool. Makes 1 cup.

MILE-HIGH STRAWBERRY PIE

A strawberry treat that can be served all year round

CRUST

¼ cup butter

2 tablespoons light brown sugar

½ cup flour

¼ cup chopped walnuts

FILLING

1 egg white

½ cup sugar

1 (10-ounce) package frozen
  sweetened strawberries and
  their juice, thawed

½ teaspoon vanilla

1½ teaspoons lemon juice

1 cup whipping cream, whipped

Sweetened whipped cream
  (garnish)

Serves 8-10.

Preheat oven to 400 degrees.

To make crust, mix butter, sugar, flour and nuts together. Spread out in flat pan. Bake, stirring often, until mixture has browned and resembles crumbs. Remove from oven and cool.

To make filling, beat egg white until frothy, using largest bowl of electric mixer. Add sugar, berries and juice, lemon juice and vanilla. Beat for 10-15 minutes or until mixture fills bowl. Fold in whipped cream.

To assemble, place crumbs in bottom of an ungreased, 9-inch springform pan. Fill pan with strawberry mixture. Cover and freeze. Serve frozen, garnished with a fresh strawberry half or a dollop of sweetened whipped cream.

CHRISTMAS BRANDINI

1 quart vanilla ice cream,
   softened

⅓ cup brandy

Serves 6.

Mix ice cream and brandy in blender.

Freeze.

Spoon into sherbet glasses and serve with Christmas cookies.

Other liqueurs, such as creme de cocoa, creme de menthe, etc., could be substituted for brandy.

Do not add more than ⅓ cup liqueur or ice cream will not freeze.

FROZEN COFFEE BOMBE

A scoop of ice cream in a party dress

4 fully rounded scoops coffee
   ice cream

¾ cup toasted flaked coconut

¼ cup coffee liqueur

Serves 4.

Roll scoops of ice cream in toasted coconut. Freeze until firm.

Just before serving, place in individual dishes and pour 1 tablespoon liqueur over top of each bombe.

TOFFEE ICE CREAM DAZZLER

4 scoops chocolate ice cream

¼ cup crushed English toffee or Heath Bar candy bar

4 ladyfinger halves

4 teaspoons dark rum

4 scoops coffee ice cream

FUDGE SAUCE

1 small (7¼-ounces) can evaporated milk

1 cup sugar

2 ounces unsweetened chocolate

1 tablespoon margarine

½ teaspoon vanilla

¼ teaspoon salt

Serves 4.

In 4 tall goblets, place a scoop of chocolate ice cream in each. Sprinkle 1 teaspoon crushed toffee on top. Lay ½ of a ladyfinger next. Spoon 1 teaspoon rum over ladyfinger. Add a scoop of coffee ice cream. Sprinkle with remaining crushed toffee.

Place in freezer. At serving time pour Fudge Sauce over the top.

To make Fudge Sauce, combine evaporated milk and sugar in a small saucepan. Place over medium heat, stirring often. Bring to a boil and boil for 1 minute. Turn heat down and add chocolate, stirring until melted. Stir in margarine, vanilla and salt. Sauce will be thin. Cool and store until ready to use.

LEMON ICE CREAM

Very appealing served in a chocolate cup

1 cup sugar

1 cup whole milk

⅓ cup fresh lemon juice

1 cup whipping cream

½ teaspoon vanilla

Mint leaves

Serves 6.

Mix sugar, milk and lemon juice.

Whip cream until stiff. Fold cream into milk mixture. Add vanilla and pour into a shallow container to freeze.

Stir at least once when partially frozen.

Garnish with fresh mint leaves or paper-thin lemon slices.

MARIONBERRY ICE CREAM

The color is like the taste—marvelous!

1 ¼ cups marionberries

1 cup sugar

1 cup whole milk

2 tablespoons fresh lemon juice

⅛ teaspoon salt

1 cup whipping cream

Serves 6-8.

Puree marionberries in a food processor. Then run through a Foley food mill or press through a fine-mesh strainer to remove seeds. (Make ¾ cup puree.)

Mix together sugar, milk, lemon juice, salt and puree.

Whip the cream until stiff. Fold the cream into the puree mixture.

Freeze in a shallow pan. Stir at least once when partially frozen.

RASPBERRY SHERBET

Simplicity at its best!

10 ounces frozen raspberries, thawed

1 cup buttermilk

½ cup sugar

Serves 4.

Combine raspberries, buttermilk and sugar in food processor or blender. Blend 15-20 seconds or until well mixed.

Transfer to a container and freeze. Stir when partially frozen.

Serve in stemmed glasses and garnish with fresh berries.

STRAWBERRY ROYALE SORBET

Eaten with guilt-free ease

20 ounces frozen sweetened
   strawberries, thawed

1 tablespoon lemon juice

¾ cup chilled ginger ale

Serves 4-5.

Blend strawberries in a food processor.
Add lemon juice and ginger ale and pulse
several times.

Pour into a container and freeze
overnight, stirring at least once.

TROPICAL FRUIT ICE

Blissfully cool and delicious!

6 ounces frozen orange juice
   concentrate, thawed

6 ounces frozen lemonade
   concentrate, thawed

3 cups crushed pineapple with
   juice

¾ cup sugar

10 ounces frozen raspberries

2 large bananas, diced

1 (12-ounce) can 7-Up

Mint leaves

Serves 12.

Mix juices, pineapple, sugar and berries in
blender. Pour into freezer container. Add
diced banana and mix well. Add 7-Up and
mix well. Cover and freeze, stirring at least
once.

Remove from freezer 30 minutes before
serving.

Serve in stemmed glasses, garnished with a
mint leaf or a fresh slice of banana.

ALMOND CRISPS

Keep this dough in your freezer for instant freshly made cookies

⅓ cup finely chopped toasted almonds

1 cup flour

½ cup packed brown sugar

¼ cup sugar

½ teaspoon baking powder

⅛ teaspoon salt

6 tablespoons chilled butter

1 large egg, beaten

½ teaspoon vanilla

Makes 5 dozen cookies.

Preheat oven to 350 degrees.

In a food processor, place almonds, flour, brown sugar, sugar, baking powder and salt. Pulse several times until well mixed. Cut butter into small chunks and add to food processor. Pulse several times until dough looks like coarse cornmeal. Combine beaten egg and vanilla and drizzle over dough. Pulse 4-5 times until barely mixed.

Form dough into rolls, 2 inches in diameter. Wrap in plastic wrap and refrigerate or freeze.

To bake, slice thinly and place on greased cookie sheet, 1½ inches apart. Bake for 8-10 minutes or until lightly browned.

ALMOND MACAROONS

This cookie got raves from our customers!

8 ounces almond paste

½ cup sugar

½ cup powdered sugar

½ teaspoon almond extract

¼ teaspoon salt

2 - 3 egg whites (⅓ cup)

Makes 25-35 macaroons.

Preheat oven to 350 degrees.

Cover baking sheets with parchment paper.

Break up almond paste and place in food processor. Blend until powdery. Add sugars, almond extract and salt. Process 1 minute. Add egg whites and blend until smooth.

Drop by teaspoonsful 2 inches apart on baking sheet. You may flatten with the back of a spoon. Bake 25-35 minutes or until a light golden brown.

Cool on baking sheet. When cold, turn upside down, moisten back of parchment paper with water and peel paper away from cookies.

MARVELOUS BROWNIES

Marvelous is an understatement for these super brownies

½ cup butter, softened

1 cup sugar

2 eggs

½ cup sifted flour

A few grains of salt

1 cup chopped walnuts

2 (1-ounce) squares
   unsweetened chocolate,
   melted

½ teaspoon vanilla

CHOCOLATE MOCHA GLAZE

½ cup whipping cream

2 teaspoons instant coffee

8 ounces semi-sweet chocolate
   chips

Makes 16 (2-inch) squares.

Preheat oven to 350 degrees. Grease 8-inch square pan.

Cream butter and add sugar gradually until mixture is soft and smooth. Add eggs one at a time, beating hard after each egg. Stir in flour and salt. Mix well. Mix in nuts, melted chocolate and vanilla.

Pour into greased pan. Bake 25-30 minutes. Do not over cook. Top should be soft when touched. Cool and cut into squares or glaze if desired.

To prepare glaze, scald cream in saucepan over medium heat (until tiny bubbles form around edge). Add instant coffee and whisk until dissolved. Add chocolate chips. After 1 minute, remove from heat. Stir until chocolate is melted and smooth.

Transfer to a bowl and set bowl in ice water for a few minutes to stop cooking. Remove from water and let stand at room temperature, stirring occasionally (do not beat). When glaze reaches room temperature, pour over brownies, using a metal spatula to smooth top. Cool for 1 hour until well set. Cut with a sharp knife (dipped in hot water to avoid pulling glaze).

CARDAMOM TEA COOKIE

A crispy accompaniment to sorbets, sherbets and ices

1 cup butter, room temperature

½ cup sugar

1 egg

1⅔ cups sifted flour

2 teaspoons baking powder

1 tablespoon cinnamon

1 teaspoon ground cardamom

1 cup chopped almonds

Makes 2½ dozen cookies.

Preheat oven to 375 degrees.

Cream butter and sugar together. Add egg and beat until light and fluffy. Combine flour, baking powder, cinnamon, cardamom and almonds. Gradually add to creamed ingredients. Mix well. Refrigerate dough.

To form cookies, roll dough into balls the size of small walnuts. Place on greased cookie sheets, about 2 inches apart. Press flat. Bake for 10-12 minutes. Remove from cookie sheets and cool on wire racks.

MINT MERINGUES

Add color to your holiday dessert tray

2 large egg whites, room temperature

¾ cup sugar

½ teaspoon peppermint extract

1 (6-ounce) package mini chocolate chips

Few drops green food coloring

Makes approximately 4 dozen meringues.

Preheat oven to 350 degrees.

Beat egg whites until foamy. Very gradually add sugar, beating until stiff but not dry. Add peppermint and drops of green food coloring, mixing well. Add just enough coloring to lightly color. Fold in chocolate chips.

Grease cookie sheet or use parchment paper. (These cookies will stick!) Spoon batter by rounded teaspoons on prepared surface.

Before you put cookies in oven, turn oven off. Do not peek. Leave in oven overnight.

CHERRY WALNUT JEWELS

CRUST

½ cup butter, softened

2 tablespoons brown sugar

1 cup sifted flour

FILLING

2 eggs

1 cup brown sugar

2 tablespoons flour

½ teaspoon salt

¼ teaspoon baking powder

1 teaspoon vanilla

1 cup chopped walnuts

16 red and green glacé
    cherries, chopped

12 dates (4 ounces), chopped

ICING

1 cup powdered sugar

2 tablespoons butter, softened

1 tablespoon lemon juice

1 tablespoon orange juice

Makes 25-36 squares.

Preheat oven to 400 degrees.

To make crust layer, cream butter and 2 tablespoons brown sugar. Add 1 cup flour and mix well. Spread into the bottom of an 8-inch square pan. Bake for 8-10 minutes until lightly browned. Reduce oven heat to 350 degrees.

To make filling, beat eggs. Add 1 cup brown sugar, 2 tablespoons flour, salt, baking powder and vanilla. Mix well. Fold in walnuts, cherries and dates. Pour over baked crust layer. Bake at 350 degrees for 30 minutes. Cool.

To make icing, gradually add powdered sugar to softened butter, then add lemon and orange juice as icing thickens. Spread over cooled filling. Cut into squares.

CHEESE CAKE COOKIES

For cheese cake aficionados!

⅓ cup butter

½ cup brown sugar

1 cup flour

½ cup chopped nuts

8 ounces cream cheese

¼ cup sugar

1 egg

2 tablespoons milk

1 tablespoon lemon juice

½ teaspoon vanilla

Yield: 16-18 rectangles

Preheat oven to 350 degrees

Cream butter and brown sugar. Add flour and nuts. Mix well. Reserve a cup of this mixture for the topping. Press remaining mixture into the bottom of an 8-inch square pan. Bake 12-15 minutes and allow to cool.

Blend sugar and cream cheese until smooth. Add milk, egg, lemon juice and vanilla. Beat well. Spread evenly over baked crust and sprinkle top with reserved crumbs. Bake 25 minutes. Cool and cut into rectangles.

CRANBERRY CHEESECAKE SQUARES

Especially colorful on a buffet table

CRUST

⅓ cup packed brown sugar

1 cup unsifted flour

½ cup chopped medium-fine walnuts

⅓ cup butter, melted

CREAM CHEESE LAYER

8 ounces cream cheese, softened

¼ cup sugar

1 egg

3 tablespoons half and half

1 tablespoon lemon juice

1 teaspoon vanilla

Makes 16 (2-inch) squares.

Preheat oven to 350 degrees.

Combine sugar, flour and walnuts. Mix well. Stir in melted butter. Pat into 8-inch square pan. Bake for 10-12 minutes.

Lower oven temperature to 325 degrees. Beat cream cheese and sugar together until light and fluffy. Add egg and beat until well blended. Add cream, lemon juice and vanilla. Blend well. Pour over baked crust and spread evenly. Bake for 15-20 minutes or until set. Chill and top with glaze.

CRANBERRY GLAZE

3 cups fresh cleaned cranberries

1 tablespoon gelatin

¼ cup cold water

1 cup sugar

½ cup red currant jelly

Makes enough for one (8-inch) cheesecake.

Soften gelatin in cold water while cleaning cranberries. Heat cranberries, sugar and jelly in stainless pan for 10 minutes, stirring occasionally. Remove from heat and stir in gelatin until dissolved. Place pan in bowl of ice and chill, stirring often.

Pour over cheesecake and let set in refrigerator for a least 1 hour before cutting. Cut with a sharp knife dipped in hot water.

GINGERBREAD BOYS

Let the kids help with these!

1 cup shortening

1 cup sugar

1 egg, beaten

1 cup molasses

2 tablespoons vinegar

5 cups sifted flour

1½ teaspoons baking soda

½ teaspoon salt

2 - 3 teaspoons ginger

1 teaspoon cinnamon

1 teaspoon ground cloves

Cinnamon candies

Makes 4-6 dozen.

Preheat oven to 375 degrees.

Thoroughly cream shortening with sugar; add beaten egg. Stir in molasses and vinegar. Beat well.

Sift together dry ingredients and stir into molasses mixture. Chill at least 3 hours.

On lightly floured surface, roll dough to ⅛-inch thickness. Cut with gingerbread-boy cutter. Place 1 inch apart on greased cookie sheet. Use cinnamon candies for faces and buttons.

Bake for 5-6 minutes (longer for larger cookies).

Cool slightly and remove from cookie sheet to a rack to cool completely.

GRAM'S DANISH COOKIES

½ pound butter, softened

1 cup sugar

2 tablespoons cold water

1 teaspoon vanilla or almond extract

3 cups sifted flour (cake flour makes a finer texture)

¼ teaspoon baking powder

Makes 8 dozen cookies.

Preheat oven to 375 degrees.

Cream butter and sugar. Add water and extract and mix well. Combine flour and baking powder. Add to creamed mixture. Mix well.

Roll in 3 rolls about 2 inches thick and 12 inches long. Chill overnight, or put in freezer for 2 hours. Slice ¼ inch thick on an angle. Place on greased cookie sheet, 1 inch apart. Bake 10-12 minutes.

LEMON BARS

Oh so lemony!

CRUST

1 cup butter

2 cups flour

½ cup powdered sugar

TOPPING

4 eggs

2 cups sugar

¼ cup flour

6 tablespoons fresh lemon juice

Grated rind of 1 lemon

1 teaspoon baking powder

⅛ teaspoon salt

Makes 40 (2-inch) bars.

Preheat oven to 350 degrees.

Combine butter, flour and powdered sugar in food processor. Pulse until well mixed. Pat into bottom of a 9 by 13-inch pan. Bake 15 minutes. Should barely be golden in color.

Beat eggs until thick and light colored; add remaining ingredients. Pour over hot crust and bake an additional 20 minutes or until set. Cool and cut into squares.

Lemon Crisps

1 cup unsalted butter, softened

1½ cups sugar

4 large egg yolks

2 tablespoons fresh lemon juice

2 teaspoons grated lemon rind

½ teaspoon lemon extract

3 cups flour

½ teaspoon salt

Makes 7 dozen cookies.

Preheat oven to 375 degrees.

Cream butter and sugar until fluffy. Add yolks, lemon juice, rind and extract. Beat until light. Mix in flour and salt until just blended.

Form into two rolls of 2 inches in diameter. Wrap in waxed paper and chill several hours. Slice between ⅛- and ¼-inch thick. (Dough can also be frozen and sliced right out of the freezer.)

Place 1½ inches apart on greased cookie sheet. Bake 8-10 minutes or until edges brown lightly.

Cookies keep 1 week at room temperature or freeze up to 3 months.

MAIDS OF HONOR

From Richmond, England, comes this marvelous tart for tea

SHORT-CRUST PASTRY

6 tablespoons chilled butter

2½ tablespoons shortening, chilled

1½ cups flour

1 tablespoon sugar

3 - 4 tablespoons ice water

FILLING

2 egg yolks

½ cup sugar

½ cup finely chopped almonds

1 tablespoon finely grated lemon peel

2 tablespoons whipping cream

1 tablespoon flour

Makes 35 mini-size tarts.

Mix butter, shortening, flour and sugar in food processor until like cornmeal. Add water and pulse a few times to begin forming a ball. Remove from processor and form into flat discs. Refrigerate for 30 minutes.

Roll pastry ⅛ inch thick. Cut 2-inch circles and gently fit into mini-muffin cups that have been lightly greased. Edge of shell should barely come to top of pan. May be frozen at this point or refrigerated for up to three days.

To make filling (enough for 30-35 mini-tart shells), beat egg yolks, sugar, almonds, lemon peel and flour until well blended. Slowly add cream and mix well.

Ladle filling into shells to within ⅛ inch of rim. For ease in removing from pan, do not overfill.

Bake at 400 degrees for approximately 8-10 minutes or until golden brown and puffed in the center. Let rest for 10 minutes. Gently remove from pan with point of paring knife.

MELTING MOMENTS

Melts in your mouth

2 cups sifted flour

1 cup butter, softened

2 tablespoons powdered sugar

FROSTING

¼ cup butter, softened

1 cup sifted powdered sugar

1 teaspoon vanilla

Makes 3-4 dozen cookies.

Do not preheat oven. Mix together ingredients and roll into small balls of ¾ inch.

Bake at 300 degrees on the highest rack of oven for 30 minutes. (Start with cold oven.)

Remove when lightly brown. Cool and frost.

To prepare frosting, mix frosting ingredients well.

RASPBERRY BARS

1¾ cups sifted flour

1 cup lightly packed brown sugar

½ teaspoon baking soda

1 cup butter, chilled

1½ cups quick cooking oatmeal

12 ounces raspberry jam

Makes 54 (1½-inch) bars.

Preheat oven to 375 degrees.

In food processor, combine flour, brown sugar and soda. Pulse to blend. Cut chilled butter into chunks, add to flour mixture and process until meal-like and thoroughly blended. Add oatmeal and pulse a few more times. (May need to divide into 2 batches if this is too much for your food processor.)

Pat scant ½ of mixture into a lightly greased 9 x 13-inch pan. Spread jam over this layer, then sprinkle remaining mixture evenly over jam.

Bake about 20 minutes. Watch edges so bars do not get too brown. Cool. Cut into bars.

ORANGE BUTTER COOKIES

1 cup butter, softened

½ cup sugar

½ cup light brown sugar

1 egg

2 tablespoons orange juice

⅛ teaspoon vanilla

2 cups sifted flour

¼ teaspoon salt

¼ teaspoon baking powder

½ cup finely chopped pecans or
   walnuts

1 tablespoon grated orange
   peel

Makes 6-7 dozen cookies.

Preheat oven to 375 degrees.

In a large bowl, beat sugars and butter until blended. Add egg and beat until fluffy. Add orange juice and vanilla.

Combine flour, salt and baking powder. Stir into the butter mixture. Stir in nuts and orange peel. Chill.

Roll dough into 2 (1¼-inch) rolls. Wrap in waxed paper and chill at least 3 hours. Slice ⅛- to ¼-inch thick. Place 1 inch apart on greased cookie sheet.

Bake 8-9 minutes until pale golden. Do not over bake. Cool on wire racks.

SCOTCH SHORTBREAD

The best shortbread has rice flour.

½ pound butter, softened

½ cup sugar

2 cups sifted flour

¼ cup rice flour

Makes 4 dozen.

Preheat oven to 325 degrees.

Mix ingredients well and pat into a 7 x 11-inch pan. Prick holes in the surface with a fork.

Bake 45-55 minutes.

While still warm, cut into squares or triangles. Cool on racks.

AMARETTO CREAM

Serve over fresh fruit or pound cake

1 cup whipping cream

1 ½ cups vanilla yogurt

1 tablespoon dark brown sugar

⅛ teaspoon almond extract

4 amaretto cookies, finely
    crushed

Makes 3 cups.

Beat whipping cream until stiff. Fold in vanilla yogurt, brown sugar and almond extract. Refrigerate.

Sprinkle amaretto cookie crumbs over the Amaretto Cream.

CHOCOLATE SAUCE

⅓ cup light corn syrup

3 tablespoons butter

1 ounce bitter chocolate

¼ cup unsweetened cocoa

¾ cup sugar

½ cup half and half

⅛ teaspoon salt

1 teaspoon vanilla

Serves 10.

Boil corn syrup about 2-3 minutes or until it strings off spoon. Set aside.

Melt butter and chocolate in a small saucepan. Sift cocoa and sugar together. Add to melted butter and chocolate. Blend well. Add corn syrup and half and half. Bring to a boil. Whip with wire whisk about 10 seconds. Remove from heat. Add salt and vanilla. Cool.

Store in refrigerator. It will not sugar.

To serve, reheat over hot water. This is delicious over ice cream.

FRENCH PASTRY CREAM

Try it in a tart shell and top with your favorite berries

6 ounces cream cheese, softened

1 cup whipping cream, unwhipped

¼ cup powdered sugar

½ teaspoon vanilla

½ teaspoon grated lemon peel

1 teaspoon fresh lemon juice

Makes 2 cups.

Beat softened cream cheese in electric mixer until smooth and creamy. Gradually add whipping cream, alternating with powdered sugar. Add flavorings. Store in refrigerator. Serve on sponge or pound cake, topped with fresh berries.

As an alternate method, combine all ingredients in a food processor, which will produce a lighter and more fluid texture.

LEMON CUSTARD SAUCE

Make-in-a-flash dessert, wonderful served over lemon sherbet or fruit

3 egg yolks

¼ cup sugar

⅛ teaspoon salt

1½ cups milk

1 teaspoon lemon extract

¼ teaspoon vanilla

Makes 1⅓ cups.

Beat egg yolks slightly. Add sugar and salt. Mix well. Place yolk mixture in top of double boiler and stir in milk. Cook over hot water, stirring constantly until mixture just coats a metal spoon. Remove pan from hot water and place in a pan of cold water. (Cooking too long will make the custard curdle). Beat in lemon and vanilla extracts. Chill before using.

BLUEBERRY SAUCE

Versatile—serve on blintzes, ice cream, pudding or cakes

1 tablespoon cornstarch

2 tablespoons sugar

2 cups fresh or frozen
   blueberries

¼ cup orange juice

¼ cup water

¼ teaspoon grated orange peel

⅛ teaspoon ground nutmeg

Dash salt

Makes about 2 cups.

Mix cornstarch with sugar, then combine all ingredients in a saucepan. Cook and stir over medium heat 4-5 minutes or until thickened.

Coconut Crumb Crust

A good base for an ice-cream pie

2 tablespoons butter

2 tablespoons sugar

¼ cup finely crushed vanilla
    wafers or graham crackers

1 ½ cups thin flaked coconut

Makes 1 crust.

Preheat oven to 350 degrees.

Cream butter and sugar. Add crumbs and coconut. Blend thoroughly and press onto the bottom and sides of a greased, 9-inch pie pan.

Bake 6-8 minutes or until lightly browned. Cool.

Basic Food Processor Pie Crust

1 ¼ cups flour

¼ teaspoon salt

¼ cup cold shortening

3 tablespoons cold butter

¼ cup cold water

Makes 1 (9-inch) crust.

Combine flour and salt in processor. Pulse to thoroughly mix. Place cold shortening and butter (in small chunks) into food processor. Pulse several times until dough is fine and crumbly and resembles finely chopped nuts. Drizzle ⅓ of the water over the surface. Pulse 4-5 times. Repeat twice more until water is gone. Stop when dough begins to gather together. Pat into a 5-inch flat round, ready to roll out.

Party Fare

The Old Kerr Nursery building and the lovely gardens are a gracious setting for private parties and celebrations on weekends and late afternoons. The Catering department reflects the same quality and careful attention to detail that is presented in the restaurant.

Each event is planned especially for the client, with a personal hostess working with each to assure a perfect occasion. The food is prepared and served by volunteers and proceeds support the programs of Albertina Kerr Centers.

Toasted Asparagus Roll-Ups

Heralding spring in the Pacific Northwest!

14 thin slices white bread, crusts removed

1 (8-ounce) package cream cheese, room temperature

8 slices bacon, fried crisp, drained and crumbled

Finely grated zest of 1 lemon

14 asparagus spears, cooked tender crisp and dried

¼ cup melted butter

Makes 28 cocktail-size or 14 tea-size rolls.

Preheat oven to 400 degrees.

Flatten bread with rolling pin. Combine cheese, bacon and lemon zest. Spread mixture evenly on each slice of bread. Place 1 asparagus spear on edge of each slice and roll. Cut in halves. Place seam side down on a lightly buttered baking sheet. Brush tops with butter.

Bake for 10 minutes or until lightly browned. Watch carefully!

Molded Avocado Pinwheel

Impressive

1 tablespoon unflavored gelatin

¼ cup cold water

1½ cups mashed avocado

1 tablespoon fresh lemon juice

1 (.6-ounce) package dry Italian salad dressing mix

2 cups sour cream

3 tablespoons chopped parsley

Dash of Tabasco

Assorted garnishes

Makes 25-30 servings.

Soften gelatin in water and heat until dissolved. Blend avocados, lemon juice and salad dressing mix in food processor until smooth. Add sour cream, parsley and Tabasco. Pulse a few times. Add dissolved gelatin. Mix.

Pour mixture into a 12-inch flan pan that has been rinsed with cold water. Cover with plastic wrap and refrigerate overnight or until firm.

Unmold on footed plate and decorate with concentric rings of assorted garnishes. Serve with bread rounds or crackers. Possible garnishes are baby shrimp, chopped green onions, cucumber (peeled, seeded and chopped), chopped ripe olives and tomato rose in center.

GINGER MINTED CARROTS

A splash of color for your antipasto tray

2 pounds of French coreless
    carrots, peeled, or 2 pounds
    carrots, peeled and cut in
    bite-sized pieces

1 cup orange juice

1 teaspoon fresh grated ginger

Salt and pepper

2 tablespoons rice vinegar

1 tablespoon chopped fresh mint

Makes about 6 cups.

Combine carrots, orange juice, ginger, salt and pepper in saucepan. Cover and bring to a boil. Simmer for 5-7 minutes or until tender crisp. Add rice vinegar. Store in covered container. Refrigerate for 6 hours or up to 1 week.

To serve, drain and arrange on a serving dish. Sprinkle with mint.

WALNUT-STUFFED MUSHROOMS

An unexpected combination

24 medium-large mushrooms

FILLING

Stems from mushrooms

¼ cup butter, for sautéing
    mushroom stems

1 cup dry bread crumbs

½ cup chopped walnuts

3 tablespoons chopped green
    onions

1½ teaspoons dried basil

¼ cup sour cream

Salt and pepper to taste

TOPPING

½ cup Parmesan cheese

¼ teaspoon paprika

Makes 24 mushrooms.

Clean mushrooms with a damp cloth and scoop out stems with a melon baller. Refrigerate mushrooms, covered with a paper towel, until ready to stuff.

Chop stems medium-fine in food processor. Sauté in butter 3-4 minutes. Cool. Add crumbs, walnuts, green onions and basil. Mix well. This may be prepared up to 2 days in advance.

Preheat oven to 350 degrees.

Add sour cream, salt and pepper to crumb mixture. Fill mushrooms so that they are nicely rounded. Dip tops in the Parmesan-paprika mixture. Place on ungreased jelly roll pan. Just before baking, pour ¾ cup water into bottom of pan. Bake 12-15 minutes or until heated through.

CHAMPIGNON AUX HERBES

Include with GINGERED MINTED CARROTS *for your buffet*

1¼ pounds medium mushrooms

¼ cup finely snipped chives

MARINADE

⅔ cup olive oil

¼ cup tarragon vinegar

¼ cup white wine vinegar

½ teaspoon finely minced garlic

1 teaspoon grated lemon rind

¼ cup chopped parsley
   (garnish)

Serves 25-30 as an hors d'oeuvre.

Wipe mushrooms clean and trim stems so they are a short, even length. Sprinkle mushrooms with chives.

Combine all ingredients for marinade. Whisk until blended and thick. Pour marinade over mushrooms, stirring until well coated. Cover and refrigerate overnight. Stir occasionally.

To serve, bring mushrooms to room temperature, drain the marinade off and arrange mushrooms in a serving dish. Sprinkle with parsley. Serve with toothpicks.

BACON POTATOES

Much-asked-for favorite at Albertina's

18-20 very small red potatoes,
   washed

1 (8-ounce) package cream cheese,
   room temperature

3 green onions, finely chopped

¼ cup Parmesan cheese

6 strips bacon, cooked, drained
   and finely crumbled

Makes 18-20 servings.

Boil potatoes in salted water until tender. Drain, cover and chill.

On day of serving, scoop out center of potatoes with a melon baller. Mix onion, cream cheese and Parmesan cheese. Fill center of potatoes with the cheese mixture. Dip top of potato in crumbled bacon. Refrigerate. When ready to serve, heat potatoes in a 250-degree oven for 10-12 minutes or until warm.

Be creative with the leftover potato balls; hashbrowns or potato salad are good possibilities.

ORZO-FILLED CHERRY TOMATOES

50 cherry tomatoes, washed

FILLING

½ cup uncooked orzo

6 green onions, finely chopped

2½ tablespoons pine nuts

2 teaspoons fresh basil or ½ teaspoon dried

2 tablespoons olive oil

1 tablespoon lemon juice

Salt and pepper to taste

Parsley (garnish)

Makes 50.

Remove a slice from the stem end of each tomato. Scoop out the pulp. Turn upside down on paper towels to drain.

To prepare filling, cook orzo according to package directions. Combine all filling ingredients, except parsley. Fill tomatoes and garnish tops with a small parsley leaf. Cover and refrigerate until serving time.

CHEESE-STUFFED CHERRY TOMATOES

Striking!

40-50 cherry tomatoes, washed

FILLING

1 (8-ounce) package cream cheese

⅓ cup crumbled bleu cheese

2 tablespoons mayonnaise

½ teaspoon Worcestershire sauce

½ teaspoon onion juice or 1 tablespoon green onion

Salt and pepper to taste

1 tablespoon cream for thinning filling

Makes 40-50.

Remove a slice from the stem end of each tomato. Scoop out pulp and turn upside down on paper towels to drain.

Combine all filling ingredients except cream, salt and pepper. Pulse in food processor until just blended, taste, add salt and pepper. Add cream, if necessary. Fill pastry bag and pipe filling into each tomato. Top with parsley or baby dill sprig. Cover and refrigerate until serving time.

CLAMS ON THE HALF SHELL

3 - 4 dozen small butter clams (2 pounds)

MARINADE

4 tablespoons olive oil

4 tablespoons fresh lemon juice

2 cloves garlic, finely minced

2 green onions, finely chopped

½ teaspoon coriander

Dash of Tabasco

Serves 8-10 as hors d'oeuvre.

Scrub and clean clams under running cold water. Place in a single layer in a large pan with ½ inch of water. Bring to a boil with lid on. Boil just until clam shells open (3-4 minutes). Discard shells that will not open. Shuck clams, saving half the shells. Clean shells and refrigerate.

Make marinade by mixing all the ingredients. Add clams and allow to marinate 24-36 hours, refrigerated.

Place 1 clam on each shell. If desired, arrange clam shells on a bed of rock salt. Garnish with parsley or baby dill. Serve very cold.

CRAB PUFFS

2 egg whites

1 cup mayonnaise

½ teaspoon curry powder

1½ cups flaked, fresh crab meat

Paprika

45 melba toast rounds or thinly sliced baguettes

Makes 45 hors d'oeuvres.

Preheat broiler and place rack 8 inches from heat element. Beat egg whites until stiff but not dry. Stir curry into mayonnaise. Fold in egg whites and then crab. Place a generous mound on each piece of toast or bread round. Sprinkle with paprika. Broil until puffy and lightly browned. Serve hot.

SALMON MOUSSE

Stunning in a fish mold

½ cup cold water

2 tablespoons unflavored gelatin

1 cup boiling water

1 cup mayonnaise

2 tablespoons fresh lemon juice

3 tablespoons finely chopped
    green onion

1 teaspoon Tabasco

½ teaspoon paprika

½ teaspoon salt

2 tablespoons capers, rinsed

2 (16-ounce) cans red salmon,
    drained, skinned and boned

½ pint whipping cream

Rye bread

Crackers

Makes 1 (6-cup) mold.

Place gelatin in cold water and let stand 10 minutes. Add boiling water. Stir until gelatin is dissolved. Cool to room temperature. Add mayonnaise, lemon juice, green onions, Tabasco, paprika, salt and capers. Taste and adjust lemon juice. Refrigerate until mixture begins to gel.

Place prepared salmon into a food processor. Pulse until fluffy. Add to gelatin mixture.

Whip cream until soft peaks form. Fold into salmon mixture.

Rinse fish mold with cold water and pour mousse into mold. Cover and refrigerate overnight. Unmold and garnish. Serve with cocktail-sized, dark rye bread or crackers.

SALMON PARTY BALL

1 (16-ounce) can red salmon

1 (8-ounce) package cream cheese, softened

1 tablespoon lemon juice

2 teaspoons finely chopped green onion

1 teaspoon prepared horseradish

¼ teaspoon salt

½ teaspoon liquid smoke

½ cup chopped pecans or filberts

Assorted crackers

Fresh dill, optional

Makes 1 (5-inch) ball.

Drain salmon. Remove skin and bones and pulse in processor until fluffy. Combine the next 6 ingredients. Mix thoroughly by hand. Blend in salmon.

Prepare a round-bottomed bowl with a double layer of plastic wrap. Mound salmon mixture into bowl. Round ball by smoothly drawing plastic up and around mixture, twisting plastic closed at top of ball. Refrigerate overnight or up to 3 days. To serve, unmold salmon ball, roll in nuts, and serve with assorted crackers. Garnish with fresh dill, if desired.

SHRIMP QUICHE

1 BASIC PIE CRUST

½ cup finely minced green onion

2 tablespoons butter

4 eggs

1 ½ cups half and half

½ teaspoon salt

½ teaspoon dill weed

¼ teaspoon cayenne pepper

1 cup small cooked shrimp

1 ½ cups grated Swiss cheese (6 ounces)

¼ cup Parmesan cheese

Makes approximately 24 small hors d'oeuvres.

Preheat oven to 350 degrees.

Place crust in bottom and half way up sides of a 9-inch square pan. Sauté green onions in butter and cool. Beat together eggs, cream, salt, dill weed and cayenne pepper. Sprinkle shrimp, Swiss cheese and green onions over bottom of pastry-lined pan. Pour egg mixture evenly over cheese and shrimp. Sprinkle top with Parmesan cheese. Bake 40-45 minutes or until small knife inserted in center of quiche comes out clean. The center should be puffed. Let stand 15-20 minutes and cut in bite-sized pieces.

These may be made in mini-muffin tins. Bake at 375 degrees for 15-20 minutes or until set.

SHRIMP BUTTERFLY DEVILED EGGS

Nestle in a bed of sprouts for an attractive presentation

12 hard-cooked eggs, peeled

½ teaspoon dill weed

¼ cup mayonnaise

1 teaspoon lemon juice

Salt and pepper to taste

24 small shrimp, cooked

24 strips pimiento

Makes 24.

Cut eggs in halves with a thin sharp knife. Remove yolks and take a small slice off bottoms of whites so they sit flat. Process or grate yolks to a fine fluffy texture. Add dill weed, mayonnaise, lemon juice, salt and pepper. Mix lightly until well blended.

Fill egg whites, leaving a smooth surface. Keep whites clean. Cut shrimp in halves lengthwise. To form butterfly, place shrimp halves on top of yolks, curving away from each other. Place a tiny strip of pimiento in center of egg between the shrimp.

CHICKEN-CHILE CHEESECAKE

Garnish this unique appetizer cheesecake with a tomato rose and sprig of parsley

CRUST

¾ cup finely crushed tortilla chips

3 tablespoons melted butter

FILLING

1½ pounds cream cheese, softened

4 large eggs

1 teaspoon chili powder

1 teaspoon Worcestershire sauce

4 tablespoons minced green onions

¼ teaspoon salt

1½ cups finely shredded, cooked chicken

8 ounces chopped green chiles, drained

1½ cups shredded Monterey Jack cheese

TOPPING

2 cups sour cream

⅛ teaspoon Tabasco

2 tablespoons finely chopped parsley

Serves 50-75 as an hors d'oeuvre.

Preheat oven to 350 degrees.

Lightly grease a 9-inch springform pan. Mix crushed chips and butter together and press in bottom of pan. Set aside.

Beat cream cheese in electric mixer at high speed until light and fluffy. Add eggs, one at a time, beating well after each addition. Add chili powder, Worcestershire sauce, salt and green onions. Blend thoroughly. Pour ½ of this mixture into pan. Combine chicken, chiles and cheese and spread evenly on top of cream cheese mixture. Carefully, pour remaining cheese mixture over chicken-chile-cheese layer. Bake for 15 minutes. Reduce heat to 300 degrees and continue baking 40-45 minutes or until set. Center will be soft. Cool on wire rack. Cover and refrigerate overnight.

To serve, unmold cheesecake on serving plate. Combine topping and spread evenly on top of cake. May be served with crackers or dark rye bread.

COCKTAIL PUFFS

One of Albertina's exceptional recipes; choose your favorite filling

PATE A CHOUX

1 cup water

½ cup butter or margarine

1 cup flour

4 eggs

SHRIMP FILLING

1 pound small salad shrimp

⅓ cup finely chopped green onions

2 teaspoons Dijon mustard

½ teaspoon dried tarragon

1 tablespoon fresh lemon juice

½ cup chopped (medium fine) water chestnuts

¾ - 1 cup mayonnaise

CURRIED CHICKEN FILLING

2 cups finely chopped, cooked chicken

¼ cup finely chopped celery

1 tablespoon chopped green onions or chives

¼ cup finely chopped peanuts

1 small tart apple, peeled, cored and coarsely grated

⅓ cup mayonnaise

2 teaspoons curry powder

Pastry makes 50 puffs and each filling makes enough to fill 50 puffs.

Preheat oven to 400 degrees.

To prepare puffs, combine water and butter in pan and bring to full rolling boil. When butter is melted, remove from heat. Add flour all at once, stirring quickly until mixture is smooth and thick and forms a ball. Cool until warm.

Place in food processor or mixing bowl. Add eggs one at a time, beating well after each addition. Scrape down and beat for additional 2 minutes.

Grease cookie sheet, rinse with cold water and drain. Drop by small teaspoonfuls 1 inch apart on cookie sheet or pipe from pastry bag. Bake at 400 degrees for 10 minutes. Reduce heat to 350 degrees and bake for 10 minutes more or until golden colored and crisp. Cool. Store in tightly covered tins or freeze.

Select filling and prepare according to directions.

Cut top third of puff almost through, leaving hinge. Remove excess membrane inside puff. When filling puffs, use 1 rounded teaspoon of filling per puff.

To make Shrimp Filling, mix all ingredients except shrimp. This may be done the day before serving. Refrigerate. When ready to serve, add shrimp to filling and gently mix. Taste and add more lemon juice and/or mayonnaise if needed. These puffs are best filled near serving time.

To make Curried Chicken Filling, combine chicken, celery, green onions and

COCKTAIL PUFFS

CHICKEN ALMOND FILLING

2 cups finely chopped, cooked chicken

2 cups mayonnaise

1½ cups grated Monterey Jack or Swiss cheese

⅔ cup finely chopped, toasted almonds

½ cup finely chopped parsley

1 cup finely chopped green onions

2 tablespoons fresh lemon juice

2 teaspoons Worcestershire sauce

Salt and pepper to taste

peanuts. (This may be done 1 day ahead.) Refrigerate. Add remaining ingredients to chicken mixture, mixing lightly to combine. Fill puffs. A small parsley bouquet with thinly sliced red and green apples makes a wonderful garnish for these puffs.

To prepare Chicken Almond Filling, preheat oven to 350 degrees. Combine all ingredients and mix thoroughly. Taste and adjust seasonings. Fill puffs and place on an ungreased cookie sheet and bake for 5 minutes, or until bubbly. Serve hot.

CHICKEN SATES

Serve with your favorite peanut sauce

2 whole chicken breasts, boned
   and skinned

25 small mushrooms

1 large green pepper, seeded

MARINADE

¼ cup oil

¼ cup Karo syrup

¼ cup soy sauce

1 clove garlic, crushed

¼ teaspoon ground ginger

Makes 50 small sates.

To prepare marinade, mix all marinade ingredients together.

Cut chicken into ½-inch cubes. Quarter the mushrooms. Cut pepper into 50 (¾-inch) squares. Pour marinade over all, cover and refrigerate overnight.

Preheat oven to 400 degrees.

Alternate marinated pieces on skewers in this order: mushroom, chicken, pepper, chicken, mushroom.

Place on baking sheet and bake for 10 minutes. Serve warm in chafing dish.

CURRIED CHICKEN CHEESECAKE

CRUST

1 ⅓ cups Keebler cracker crumbs

¼ cup melted butter

FILLING

1 ½ teaspoons instant chicken
    bouillon granules

1 tablespoon boiling water

1 ½ pounds cream cheese,
    softened

3 eggs

1 cup sour cream

3 tablespoons grated onion

3 tablespoons finely minced
    celery

1 tablespoon flour

1 tablespoon curry powder

¼ teaspoon salt

1 ½ cups finely chopped, cooked
    chicken

½ cup slivered almonds, toasted

⅓ cup golden raisins

TOPPING

1 cup sour cream

1 ½ teaspoons curry powder

⅛ teaspoon ginger

⅓ cup chopped red pepper

⅓ cup slivered almonds, toasted

Serves 50-75 as an hors d'oeuvre.

Preheat oven to 350 degrees.

Lightly grease a 9-inch springform pan.
Mix crumbs and butter together and press
in bottom of pan. Set aside.

Dissolve chicken bouillon in boiling
water. Set aside.

Beat cream cheese in an electric mixer at
high speed until light and fluffy. Add eggs,
one at a time, beating after each addition.
Add chicken bouillon, sour cream, onions,
celery, flour, curry powder and salt. Blend
thoroughly. Stir in chicken, almonds and
raisins. Pour into prepared pan. Bake for
15 minutes. Reduce heat to 300 degrees
and continue baking 40-45 minutes or
until set. Center will be soft. Cool on wire
rack. Cover and refrigerate overnight.

To serve, unmold cheesecake on serving
plate. Combine sour cream, curry powder
and ginger. Spread evenly over top of
cake. Sprinkle chopped pepper and
slivered almonds on top. May be served
with crackers or thinly sliced baguette.

CURRIED TURKEY APPETIZERS

A wonderful use for leftover turkey

1 cup mayonnaise

1 teaspoon soy sauce

1 tablespoon fresh grated
   ginger

2 teaspoons curry powder

1 pound cooked turkey breast,
   cut in ¾-inch cubes

3 cups chopped, toasted
   almonds

Makes 50 cubes.

Mix mayonnaise, soy sauce, ginger and
curry. Roll turkey cubes in mixture and
then in almonds. Cover and refrigerate
overnight or up to 2 days.

Serve on toothpicks.

CHICKEN INDIAN CURRY BALL

Very attractive served on a bed of parsley

1 (8-ounce) package cream cheese

¼ cup mayonnaise

2 cups medium chopped cooked
   chicken

2 cups chopped, toasted
   almonds

½ teaspoon salt

4 teaspoons curry powder

5 tablespoons finely chopped
   chutney

½ cup angel coconut, toasted
   golden brown

Makes 1 (5-inch) ball to serve 15-20.

Combine all ingredients except coconut.
Line a round-bottomed bowl,
approximately 5 inches in diameter, with
double plastic wrap. Mound mixture into
bowl. Round ball by smoothly drawing
plastic up and around mixture, twisting
plastic closed at top of ball. Refrigerate for
up to 2 days. An hour before serving,
unmold and reshape, as needed, to make
ball round. Roll in toasted coconut. Serve
with crackers.

CAJUN CHICKEN MORSELS

A little effort but well worth it

1½ cups flour

1 cup finely chopped pecans

1 tablespoon oregano

2 teaspoons ground cumin

1 teaspoon dried thyme

½ teaspoon cayenne pepper

½ teaspoon salt

4 whole chicken breasts, boned, skinned and cut in 1-inch pieces

1 cup butter

Chopped parsley, garnish

MUSTARD SAUCE

4 ounces dry mustard

1 cup sugar

1 cup white wine vinegar

6 eggs, beaten

Makes 70 pieces.

Combine all ingredients except chicken, butter and parsley. Melt ⅓ cup of the butter. Dip chicken pieces in butter and then in flour mixture, pressing to coat well. Refrigerate.

Halve the remaining ⅔ cup of butter and melt in a large skillet on medium heat. Add ½ of the chicken pieces and sauté until brown on all sides. Repeat with remaining butter and chicken. If not serving immediately, chicken may be wrapped in foil and refrigerated at this point. Reheat in partially opened foil in 350-degree oven for 15-20 minutes.

Place in chafing dish and sprinkle with chopped parsley. May be served with Mustard Sauce for dipping if desired.

To prepare Mustard Sauce, mix and cook sauce ingredients in double boiler until thick. Stir often while cooking.

CHICKEN STRUDEL

FILLING

2½ cups diced cooked chicken

1 medium onion, chopped

2 tablespoons olive oil

10 ounces frozen chopped
    spinach, thawed and
    squeezed dry

½ pound Munster cheese,
    grated

2 tablespoons dry white wine

⅛ teaspoon salt

¼ teaspoon black pepper

¼ teaspoon nutmeg

¼ teaspoon Worcestershire
    sauce

1 egg, slightly beaten

PASTRY

⅔ cup finely ground bread
    crumbs

½ teaspoon paprika

1 (16-ounce) package phyllo
    pastry sheets

1 cup melted butter

Makes 4 rolls, 10 slices per roll.

To prepare filling, sauté onions in oil until tender. Add chicken, spinach, cheese, wine, seasonings and egg. Mix well. Refrigerate.

Mix bread crumbs and paprika. Set aside.

Preheat oven to 375 degrees.

To assemble strudel, unfold phyllo and place on tray or baking sheet. Cover with waxed paper and a lightly dampened cloth. Layer 5 sheets of phyllo, brushing each sheet with butter and sprinkling each with crumb mixture (approx. 1½ teaspoon per sheets). Spoon ¼ of chicken mixture ½ inch down from the top edge of the short side. Roll like a jelly roll, placing seam side down on an ungreased cookie sheet. Brush top with butter. Cut diagonal slashes halfway through the roll at 1-inch intervals. Repeat process until all phyllo and filling is used. Bake for 10-15 minutes or until golden and crispy.

Cut through the slashes and serve.

CHICKEN PHYLLO ROLLS

These wonderful little appetizers can be made 1 day before baking or stored frozen, unbaked, for up to 3 months

2½ cups medium chopped cooked chicken breasts (1½ breasts)

¾ cup mayonnaise

½ cup finely chopped green onions

1 tablespoon lemon juice

1 clove garlic, minced

1 teaspoon tarragon

Salt and pepper to taste

12 sheets phyllo

Butter, melted for brushing phyllo

Makes 24-32 rolls.

Preheat oven to 400 degrees.

To make filling, mix together chicken, mayonnaise, onions, lemon juice, garlic, tarragon, salt and pepper.

Place phyllo on cutting board and cut in half lengthwise and crosswise in six or eight equal rectangles. Keep phyllo covered with waxed paper and a damp towel while working on individual stacks.

Stack 3 sheets of phyllo, brushing each sheet with butter. Place filling at one end and roll over once. Fold in sides and continue rolling. It will resemble a fat cigar.

Place phyllo rolls on baking tray with a 1½-inch space between rolls. Bake for 8 minutes or until golden.

Orange Muffins with Smoked Turkey

½ cup butter

1 cup sugar

2 eggs

1 cup buttermilk

2 cups flour

1 teaspoon baking soda

1 cup currants

1 orange

Filling

1 cup sour cream

½ teaspoon Dijon mustard

½ pound thinly sliced
   smoked turkey breast

Makes 30-35 mini muffins.

Preheat oven to 375 degrees.

Cream butter and sugar until light and fluffy. Add eggs and continue beating. Sift flour and soda together. Add flour mixture and buttermilk to butter-egg mixture. Mix only until flour disappears. Do not over mix. Grate orange rind and squeeze juice. Reserve juice. Gently fold currants and orange rind into muffin batter.

Fill greased mini-muffin pans ⅔ full. Bake 10-15 minutes or until golden brown. Remove from tins, cool slightly and brush top of muffins with reserved orange juice. Cool completely. Muffins may be frozen at this time.

Blend sour cream and mustard. To assemble, slice muffins horizontally and spread each half with a thin layer of sour cream-mustard mixture. Place 2-3 pieces of turkey between the halves.

Cover with plastic wrap and refrigerate until ready to serve.

CANTONESE PORK

One of Albertina's exceptional recipes

2 pounds whole pork tenderloin,
  trimmed of excess fat

MARINADE

¼ cup sugar

2 tablespoons catsup

¼ cup sherry

1 teaspoon Chinese barbecue
  sauce

½ teaspoon ground ginger

2 tablespoons soy sauce

½ teaspoon salt

¼ teaspoon freshly ground
  pepper

1 clove garlic, finely minced

HOT MUSTARD

¼ cup dry mustard

1½ tablespoons Chablis

Water

Toasted sesame seeds

Makes approximately 70-80 thin slices.

Combine marinade ingredients in a stainless or glass container. Add tenderloins and marinate for 8 hours or up to 2 days. Turn occasionally.

Preheat oven to 350 degrees. Place meat on rack in baking pan. Pour 1 cup water into bottom of pan. Bake 45 minutes, basting every 15 minutes with the marinade. Turn meat over with each basting. When done, juices should run light pink when poked with knife in thickest part of tenderloin.

Let meat cool about 15 minutes. Slice thin. Serve warm or at room temperature. Accompany with Hot Mustard and toasted sesame seeds.

To prepare Hot Mustard, mix dry mustard with Chablis, adding enough water to make a dipping consistency.

Chutney-Glazed Meatballs

Meatballs

⅓ pound bulk pork sausage

¾ pound lean ground beef

½ teaspoon salt

½ teaspoon dry mustard

½ teaspoon crushed coriander seeds

¼ teaspoon allspice

1 egg, lightly beaten

¼ cup fine dry bread crumbs

¼ cup finely sliced green onions

Glaze

½ cup apple jelly

½ cup Major Grey's Chutney

1 tablespoon lemon juice

Makes 5 dozen.

Preheat oven to 450 degrees.

Up to 2 days in advance, mix meats, seasonings, egg, crumbs and onion until well blended. Shape in 1-inch balls. Place on greased metal baking trays. Bake for 5 minutes or until brown. Drain and refrigerate in covered container.

On day of serving, prepare glaze. Blend jelly, chutney and lemon juice in food processor until smooth. Place glaze in a large skillet and add meatballs. Simmer 5-8 minutes or until barely heated. Serve in chafing dish.

WINE-GLAZED SAUSAGE CHUNKS

A Superbowl Sunday knock out

1 pound Polish sausage
   (kielbasa)

1 cup dry white wine

1 tablespoon Dijon mustard

2 tablespoons Major Grey's
   Chutney, finely chopped

Chopped parsley

Serves 10 as hors d'oeuvres (approximately 50 chunks).

Slice sausage ¾ inch thick, removing skin, if possible. Cut crosswise if too large for bite size.

In a large frying pan, blend wine, mustard and chutney. Bring to a boil; add sausages and simmer until liquid is reduced and syrupy (10-15 minutes).

Place in preheated chafing dish. Sprinkle with parsley.

Rich Pastry for Quiche

This crust may be stored in refrigerator for 5 days or frozen

1 cup butter, softened

1 cup small curd cottage cheese

2 cups all-purpose flour

Makes 2 (8-inch) round quiche crusts or 1 (9 by 13-inch) rectangular crust.

Combine butter and cottage cheese in food processor or mixing bowl. Process or beat until well blended. Add flour and mix thoroughly. Roll into desired shape.

If frozen or refrigerated, let dough come to room temperature before rolling.

Colorful Vegetable Quiche

Add a bright spot to your buffet table

1 recipe Basic Pie Crust

½ cup finely chopped green onions, including some tops

2 tablespoons butter

1½ cups finely chopped peppers, combination of red, yellow and green

1½ cups half and half

4 eggs

½ teaspoon salt

¼ teaspoon cayenne pepper

½ teaspoon dill weed

1½ cups grated Swiss or Monterey Jack cheese (6 ounces)

Makes 24 small hors d'oeuvres (approximately).

Preheat oven to 375 degrees.

Place crust in a 9-inch square pan or quiche pan.

Sauté green onions in butter until barely done. Combine onions and peppers. Set aside.

Beat together half and half, eggs, salt, cayenne pepper and dill weed.

Sprinkle cheese over bottom of pastry-lined pan. Scatter vegetables evenly over the cheese. Pour egg mixture over cheese and vegetables. Bake for 15 minutes, then lower temperature to 350 degrees and bake for 25 minutes more, or until set and puffed in center. Allow to cool 15-20 minutes. Cut in bite-sized pieces or wedges.

NUTTY BRIE WITH TIPSY FRUIT

Friends, conversation and warm Brie in front of a crackling fire

½ cup dried cranberries

¼ cup dry white wine

⅓ cup chopped pecans

¼ cup butter

1 kilo Brie

Crackers or baguette

Serves 25-40.

Soak cranberries in wine overnight. Drain before garnishing.

Preheat oven to 325 degrees.

Toast pecans in butter. Set aside.

Cover a cardboard circle the size of Brie with foil. Place Brie on this circle and set both on a cookie sheet. Bake for 8-10 minutes or until barely soft inside.

To serve, arrange cranberries and pecans, separately, on top of Brie in several slightly irregular triangles. Let stand 15 minutes before placing Brie and cardboard on serving dish. (A footed cake place is attractive.) Serve with crackers or thinly sliced baguette.

Baked Brie Wrapped in Phyllo

1 kilo Brie

11 sheets phyllo

1 pound butter, melted

Crackers

Serves 25-40.

Preheat oven to 350 degrees.

Unfold phyllo. Place on tray or cookie sheet. Cover with waxed paper and a lightly dampened cloth.

Cut a piece of cardboard the size of the Brie. Cover cardboard with foil. Place on baking sheet.

To make bottom crust, prepare 5 single sheets of phyllo by brushing each sheet with butter and stacking 1 on top of the other. Work rapidly; if a sheet isn't perfectly flat, it makes no difference. Set the Brie in the middle of bottom crust. Carefully, fold phyllo around Brie, pleating the phyllo up over the sides and onto top of Brie. Remove any excess bulky pieces of phyllo so that, overall, the top is fairly flat.

To prepare the top crust, butter and stack additional 5 sheets of phyllo. Butter top and side of Brie before centering top crust on Brie. Carefully, tuck top crust around sides and under Brie and bottom crust. Remove any excess bulky phyllo. Butter entire Brie. Place on foil-lined cardboard.

Fold the last sheet of phyllo in half, lengthwise, and then into thirds, lengthwise. Beginning at 1 end, ruffle up the phyllo like a cabbage rose. Place in the middle of the Brie. Carefully, brush with butter. At this point, Brie may be refrigerated for up to 2 days.

Bake for 20-30 minutes or until the phyllo is golden brown. Let stand for 30 minutes before serving. Place Brie and cardboard on serving dish (A footed cake plate is very attractive.) Serve with assorted crackers.

WALNUT CHEESE TARTS

Make-ahead mini tarts

1 cup walnuts, roasted

4 slices lean bacon

4 green onions, finely chopped

2 cups grated Swiss cheese

3 eggs, lightly beaten

½ teaspoon salt

¼ teaspoon nutmeg

Dash cayenne pepper

2 cups half and half

32 pastry-lined, 1½-inch tart
  shells, unbaked

Makes 32 tarts.

Preheat oven to 350 degrees.

Toast walnuts in a shallow pan for 10-12 minutes. Cool and chop, medium coarse.

Increase oven temperature to 425 degrees.

Fry bacon until crisp. Drain on paper towels and crumble into small pieces. Reserve small amount of the bacon fat and sauté onions until translucent.

Combine walnuts, grated cheese, onions and bacon. Mix thoroughly. Divide mixture among shells, about a rounded tablespoon per shell.

Add spices and half and half to eggs. Whisk together. Pour over cheese mixture in pastry shells. Wipe edges of pastry free from egg mixture. These puff up in baking, so do not fill to top of pastry. Bake for 10-12 minutes or until filling is set.

Tarts freeze well. Thaw overnight in refrigerator and rewarm at 325 degrees for about 5 minutes.

CHEESE MUSHROOM FINGERS

Excellent vegetable quiche-like hors d'oeuvre without a crust. Use for brunch or buffet.

¼ cup butter

½ pound mushrooms, finely sliced

1 medium onion, chopped

1 clove garlic, minced

1 small green pepper, chopped

5 eggs, beaten

¼ cup flour

½ teaspoon baking powder

1 cup small curd cottage cheese

2 cups shredded Monterey Jack cheese

½ teaspoon nutmeg

½ teaspoon dry basil

½ teaspoon salt

Makes 50 (1 by 2-inch) fingers.

Preheat oven to 350 degrees.

Melt butter and sauté mushrooms, onions and garlic until mushrooms are slightly soft. Add green pepper and sauté one minute more. Cool. At this point, vegetables may be stored in refrigerator overnight.

Combine eggs, flour, baking powder, cheeses, nutmeg, basil and salt. Add to mushroom mixture, mixing thoroughly. Pour into a well-buttered, 10-inch square pan.

Bake for 25 minutes or until set. Cool for 15 minutes.

Cut in finger-sized pieces. Serve warm or at room temperature.

PESTO CHEESECAKE

A summer or fall favorite when basil is abundant

CRUST

¾ cup fine dry bread crumbs

⅓ cup finely chopped pine nuts

¼ cup grated Parmesan cheese

3 tablespoons melted butter

FILLING

¾ cup pesto (see LAYERED CHEESE TORTA or a quality commercial pesto)

1½ pounds cream cheese, room temperature

3 eggs

¼ cup milk

TOPPING

1 cup sour cream

1 tablespoon finely chopped parsley

2 drops Tabasco

Serves 25-40 as an hors d'oeuvre.

Preheat oven to 300 degrees.

Combine crust ingredients. Press on bottom and 1 inch up sides of lightly greased, 8-inch springform pan. Set aside.

Beat softened cream cheese at high speed in mixer until light and fluffy. Add eggs, one at a time, beating thoroughly after each addition. Add milk and pesto. Blend well and taste for additional seasonings; adjust. Pour into crumb-lined springform pan.

Bake for 50-60 minutes. Center will be soft. Turn off oven, partially open door, and leave one hour.

Remove and cool to room temperature. Wrap in 2 layers of plastic wrap and refrigerate up to 3 days.

To serve, unmold on serving plate. (A footed cake plate is attractive.) Combine topping ingredients and spread on top of cake.

Garnish with pine nuts and a sprig of basil.

HERBED CHEESE ROUNDS

¾ cup butter

½ cup grated sharp cheddar cheese

½ cup crumbled bleu cheese

2 cups flour

1½ teaspoons caraway seeds

1 clove garlic, minced

2 tablespoons chopped chives

Ripe olives, sliced (garnish)

Makes approximately 6-7 dozen.

Blend butter and cheese in mixer until smooth. Stir in flour, caraway seeds, garlic and chives and mix well. Shape in a log about 20 inches long and 1¼ inches in diameter. Wrap in a sleeve of waxed paper and seal in plastic wrap. Chill or freeze.

Preheat oven to 375 degrees.

To bake, cut in ¼-inch slices and place 1 inch apart on an ungreased baking sheet. Press olive slice in center. Bake 10-12 minutes or until golden brown.

BENGAL BOMBE

1 pound cream cheese, room temperature

¼ cup sour cream

1 cup chopped peanuts

¾ cup currants

¾ cup chopped green onions, mostly tops

2 tablespoons curry powder

½ cup Bengal hot chutney, garnish

⅓ - ½ cup chopped peanuts garnish

Makes about 4 cups.

Mix cream cheese and sour cream together in processor until creamy smooth. Add nuts, currants, green onions and curry powder and mix by hand. Form into large ball and refrigerate overnight. This may be prepared up to 2 days ahead.

To serve, place on serving platter. Pour ½ cup chutney over the top. Sprinkle with additional chopped peanuts and serve with crackers.

LAYERED CHEESE TORTA

This red, green and white-striped tower is festive for the holidays

PESTO LAYER

3 - 4 cloves garlic

2½ cups lightly packed fresh
   basil

1 cup freshly grated Parmesan
   cheese

¼ cup pine nuts

⅓ cup olive oil

Salt and pepper

SUN-DRIED TOMATO LAYER

1 (10½-ounce) jar sun-dried
   tomatoes

MASCARPONE

1 pound unsalted butter, room
   temperature

1 pound cream cheese, room
   temperature

Dark rye bread or crackers

MATERIALS NEEDED

2 18-inch squares cheesecloth

1 2-pound (6 cups) cylindrical
   container or

2 1-pound (3 cups each)
   cylindrical containers

Makes 6 cups.

To prepare Pesto Layer, drop cloves of garlic down tube of processor while it is running. Add basil, pine nuts and cheese, and process until well mixed.

Slowly add olive oil while processor is running. Pesto should have a good spreading consistency. Season with salt and pepper. Makes 1 cup.

To prepare Sun-Dried Tomato Layer, drain tomatoes, reserving 2 tablespoons of oil. Process tomatoes with oil until smooth and of spreading consistency.

To prepare Mascarpone, blend butter until light and fluffy in food processor. Cut cream cheese into 1-inch cubes and gradually add to butter. Blend until very smooth.

Moisten squares of cheesecloth with water and wring dry. Lay flat, one on top of the other. Smoothly line 2-pound container, letting edges of cloth fall outside of mold.

Make even layers of cheese-butter mixture and thin layers of pesto and tomato filling. Begin and end with cheese-butter mixture. Alternate the green and red layers to achieve a white-green/white-red striped effect. Fold cheesecloth over the top and press down lightly.

Chill overnight. Unmold and remove cheesecloth (to prevent bleeding of colors). Wrap in plastic wrap. May be made ahead and refrigerated up to 1 week.

To serve, unwrap torta and garnish with fresh basil leaves and a tomato rose. Offer dark rye bread and/or crackers.

ARTICHOKE FLAN

Make ahead and refrigerate

1 pie crust (in 9 by 13-inch baking dish)

1 pound cream cheese, room temperature

⅔ cup sour cream

¼ cup crumbled bleu cheese

3 tablespoons butter, room temperature

3 eggs

3 tablespoons chopped parsley

1 tablespoon chopped fresh dill or 1 teaspoon dried

Pinch of thyme or marjoram

Salt and pepper

1 (8½-ounce) can artichoke hearts, drained and coarsely chopped

½ cup sour cream, approximately (garnish)

Sprig of fresh dill (garnish)

Makes approximately 50 hors d'oeuvres.

Preheat oven to 375 degrees.

Combine cheeses, ⅔ sour cream and butter in processor or mixing bowl. Blend well. Add eggs and herbs. Mix well.

Spread artichokes in pastry-lined pan. Pour cheese mixture on top of artichokes. Bake for 30 minutes. Cool. Slice in bite-sized squares and garnish each piece with a bit of sour cream and a sprig of fresh dill.

Mandarin Orange and Cream Cheese Tea Sandwich on Nut Bread

¾ pound cream cheese, room temperature

1 tablespoon frozen concentrated orange juice

1 tablespoon orange zest

Mandarin orange slices, well drained

Currant jelly, heated

Dark Nut Bread

2 eggs, well beaten

1 cup sugar

¼ cup melted shortening

⅔ cup light molasses

1 cup sour milk

1½ cups white flour

½ teaspoon salt

1 teaspoon baking soda

1½ cups graham flour or whole-wheat flour

1½ cups chopped walnuts

Makes 80-90 rectangular open-faced sandwiches.

Slice chilled nut bread in ⅜ to ½-inch slices. Remove crust if too crisp. Cut in even rectangular shapes (4 per slice).

Beat cream cheese until smooth. Add orange juice and zest. Blend but do not over mix.

Spread an even layer of cream cheese on bread. Keep cut edges clean. Place Mandarin orange slice in center of frosted rectangle. Spoon a little currant jelly over orange. Refrigerate in a single layer until ready to serve.

To prepare 1 loaf Dark Nut Bread, beat eggs and sugar together until thick. Add melted shortening and molasses and beat thoroughly. Mix in sour milk. Sift white flour, salt and soda together. Add white-flour mixture and graham flour to egg mixture. Beat just until smooth (do not over mix). Fold in nuts. Pour into well-greased, 5½ by 10½-inch loaf pan or equivalent. Bake at 350 degrees for 1 hour or until bread tests done with a toothpick.

To make sour milk: Mix one tablespoon vinegar with milk to equal one cup.

CHICKEN SURPRISE TEA SANDWICH

All of these flavors add up to one good sandwich

1 cup coarsely chopped,
    cooked chicken

½ cup chopped dates

¼ cup finely chopped celery

¼ cup chopped hazelnuts

¼ cup bacon bits

½ cup mayonnaise

Whipped butter

Sandwich bread, thinly sliced

Makes approximately 2 cups of filling.

Combine chicken, dates, celery, hazelnuts and bacon bits. Mix well. Add enough mayonnaise for a moist spreading consistency. You may need to adjust the flavor with a small amount of orange juice and salt.

Spread sandwich bread with whipped butter and a generous amount of filling. (A homemade dark bread is very delicious with this filling.) Wrap sandwiches in plastic. Prepare storage container by lining it with a lightly dampened tea towel. Pack sandwiches inside. Refrigerate. Trim crusts and cut in attractive shapes before serving

OLIVE NUT TEA SANDWICH

Great contrast in color and texture

1½ cups chopped black olives

¾ cup chopped walnuts

½ cup mayonnaise

Whipped butter

Sandwich bread, thinly sliced

Makes about 2 cups of filling.

Process olives and nuts separately to medium fine. Combine with just enough mayonnaise to moisten.

Spread sandwich bread with whipped butter and spread with a generous amount of filling. (This sandwich is particularly good with 2 white-bread slices and 1 whole-wheat slice in the middle.) Wrap sandwiches in plastic. Prepare storage container by lining it with a lightly dampened tea towel. Pack sandwiches inside. Refrigerate. Trim crusts and cut in triangles before serving.

WATERCRESS TEA SANDWICH

Essentially English

¾ cup finely chopped
    watercress leaves

¼ cup finely chopped parsley

1 pound cream cheese, room
    temperature

1 tablespoon finely chopped
    green onion

Dash of lemon juice

Salt and pepper to taste

Whipped butter

Sandwich bread

Makes about 2 cups of filling.

Prepare watercress and parsley in processor. Set aside. Process cream cheese until smooth. Add watercress, parsley, green onions, lemon juice, salt and pepper. Process until well blended.

Spread sandwich bread with whipped butter and a generous layer of watercress filling. These are very attractive rolled in pinwheel shapes (trim crusts before rolling) or made in 2-3 layer sandwiches.

Wrap sandwiches in plastic. Line storage container with a lightly dampened towel and pack sandwiches inside. Refrigerate overnight. Trim crusts and cut in desired shapes before serving.

Herb Curry Dip with Capers

1 cup mayonnaise

½ cup sour cream

1 teaspoon crushed salad herbs
(mix of tarragon, basil,
thyme, marjoram and
spearmint)

⅛ teaspoon salt

¼ - ½ teaspoon curry powder

1 tablespoon chopped parsley

1 tablespoon grated onion or
finely chopped green onion

1½ teaspoons fresh lemon juice

½ teaspoon Worcestershire
sauce

2 teaspoons drained capers,
rinsed in cold water

Makes approximately 1½ cups.

Blend all ingredients. Chill well for up to
3 days. Serve with assorted raw seasonal
vegetables.

Herb Dip

Especially nice served with raw vegetables

½ pound cream cheese, room
temperature

1 cup mayonnaise

1 cup sour cream

3 tablespoons lemon juice

½ tablespoon dill weed

½ cup finely chopped green
onions, including some tops

½ cup finely chopped parsley

Salt and pepper to taste

Makes 1 quart.

Mix cream cheese by hand or in a food
processor. Add mayonnaise and blend
thoroughly. Add lemon juice and sour
cream, mixing only until blended. Stir in
dill weed, green onions and parsley. Taste
and add salt and pepper if needed.

Refrigerate at least 2 hours or overnight.

HUMMUS

The Middle East brings us this healthy low-fat dip

1 (15½-ounce) can garbanzo
    beans

3 tablespoons tahini

⅓ cup lemon juice

1 large clove garlic, finely
    chopped

⅛ teaspoon cumin

½ teaspoon salt

Water

Parsley, finely chopped (garnish)

Pita, cut up (optional)

Raw vegetables (optional)

Makes 3-4 cups.

Drain and rinse beans. Save 4-5 for
garnish. Place beans, tahini, lemon juice,
garlic, cumin and salt in food processor.
Add cold water to just below top level of
beans. Process until smooth. Taste and add
more lemon juice and salt if needed.
Refrigerate.

To serve, place in bowl and garnish with
chopped parsley and small mound of
whole beans. Serve with cut-up pieces of
pita bread and assorted raw vegetables.

LAYERED ARTICHOKE CHEESE DIP

This may be made a day ahead

1 (8½-ounce) can water-packed
    artichoke hearts, drained

1 (6-ounce) jar marinated
    artichoke hearts, drained

1 (4-ounce) can diced green
    chiles

6 tablespoons mayonnaise

6 ounces grated sharp cheddar
    cheese

Tortilla chips

Makes 2½ cups.

Preheat oven to 350 degrees.

Grease a shallow, oven-proof serving dish,
approximately 7½ by 11½ inches.

In a food processor, or by hand, chop all
the artichokes to a medium-coarse texture.
Place in greased serving dish. Scatter
chiles over the artichokes and then spread
with mayonnaise. Sprinkle cheddar cheese
on top.

Refrigerate or bake covered with foil until
heated through (approximately 15
minutes). Serve surrounded by tortilla
chips.

RED BELL PEPPER DIP

This is nice served with blue tortilla chips or crackers

4 large red peppers (1½ - 1¾ pounds)

⅓ cup butter

1 small onion, finely chopped

1 clove garlic, minced

¼ teaspoon ground cumin

Dash of cayenne pepper

1 tablespoon lemon juice

¼ teaspoon salt

1 teaspoon grated lemon peel

1½ teaspoons unflavored gelatin

¼ cup dry vermouth

½ cup whipping cream

Makes 3½-4 cups.

Reserve 2-3 rings of pepper for garnish. Seed and chop remaining peppers.

Melt butter over medium heat and add onion and pepper. Cook 10-15 minutes or until soft. Add garlic, cumin, cayenne, lemon juice and salt. Transfer to food processor and process until smooth. Place in a large bowl and blend in lemon peel.

In a small bowl, soften gelatin in vermouth for 5 minutes. Dissolve over medium heat. Stir gelatin into pepper mixture and refrigerate until it begins to set. Whip cream to soft peaks and fold into pepper mixture. Cover and refrigerate at least 2 hours or until set.

Serve in bowl garnished with pepper rings.

ALBERTINA'S CHAMPAGNE PUNCH

PUNCH BASE

1 quart orange juice or lemonade, for ice ring mold

2 cups water

1 (6-ounce) can frozen lemonade concentrate

1 (6-ounce) can frozen orange juice concentrate

2 cups apricot nectar

3 cups apple juice

2 cups unsweetened pineapple juice

1 quart ginger ale, chilled

Champagne, chilled

Makes 26 (4-ounce) glasses.

To make ice ring mold, or other shape, freeze 1 quart juice or lemonade in mold 2-3 days before needed.

To make punch base, combine water and juices. Refrigerate up to 2 days ahead.

To serve, place frozen ice ring mold in bowl and add 6 cups of punch base. Add ginger ale and 1 fifth champagne. Do not stir. Ladling will blend liquids.

For a stronger punch, add 2 fifths of champagne. This will serve 33 (4-ounce) glasses.

GALA TOMATO PUNCH

This unusual punch is beautiful garnished with lemon slices and fresh herbs

2 quarts canned beef consommé, divided in half

4 quarts tomato juice

1/3 cup fresh lemon juice

3 tablespoons Worcestershire sauce

Fresh ground pepper to taste

Tabasco to taste

Garlic (for rubbing bowl)

Makes 40 (4-ounce) glasses.

Make frozen ring mold by freezing 1 quart consommé in ring mold, or other shape, 2-3 days before needed.

Combine remaining 1 quart of consommé and juices. Add all spices except garlic. Refrigerate up to 2 days.

To serve, rub punch bowl with cut garlic. Place consommé ice ring in bowl and add the punch mixture. Stir gently.

PINK PARTY PUNCH

2 quarts cranberry juice
   cocktail, divided in half

2 cups unsweetened pineapple
   juice

½ cup lemon juice

1 (6-ounce) can frozen
   lemonade concentrate

3 quarts ginger ale, chilled

Makes 36 (4-ounce) glasses.

Make ring mold by freezing 1 quart cranberry juice in mold 2-3 days ahead.

To make punch base, mix remaining 1 quart cranberry juice, pineapple and lemon juices and lemonade together. This base may be prepared 2 days ahead and refrigerated.

If using small punch bowl, place frozen ring mold in bowl and add 3½ cups of base and 1½ quarts of ginger ale. This may be refilled once. Do not stir.

If using large punch bowl, place frozen ring mold in bowl and add all of the base and 3 quarts of ginger ale. Do not stir.

WASSAIL

Float Lady apples on top for a special look

1 gallon apple cider

4 cinnamon sticks

¾ teaspoon freshly grated
   nutmeg

8 whole cloves

9 tablespoons lemon juice

4 cups pineapple juice

2⅔ cups orange juice

Makes 42 (4-ounce) cups

Combine all ingredients in pan (do not use aluminum pan). Bring to boil and simmer 30 minutes.

To serve, strain out whole spices and pour into a pre-warmed punch bowl.

Index

Albertina Kerr Centers is one of the largest private, non-profit human services organizations in Oregon, serving clients from more than 21 counties throughout the State. Programs include residential, employment and alternative-to-employment services for people with severe developmental disabilities; psychiatric day and residential treatment for severely emotionally disturbed children; early intervention for at-risk children; outpatient counseling; and adoption and foster care for children with special needs.

Residential services include more than a dozen group homes, each serving five individuals with severe disabilities. Supervised apartment living is also available for young adults who are ready for that level of independence.

Albertina Kerr Centers have impacted thousands of lives and have provided the only home many young adults with developmental disabilities have ever known.

Notes

Notes

Notes

Notes